The Dalai Lama, Mikhail Gorbachev, Mario Vargas Llosa, Muhammad Yunus, Deepak Chopra, Federico Mayor Zaragoza, Desmond Tutu, Jean S. Bolen, Sogyal Rinpoche, Michael Douglas, Sir Richard Branson, John Berger & Others

The Art of Living

A Practical Guide to Being Alive

Edited by Claire Elizabeth Terry

editorial Kairós

Editorial Kairós S.A.
Numancia 117-121, 08029 Barcelona, Spain
To express your thoughts and for more information about *The Art of Living*,
please click on www.editorialkairos.com

Nirvana Libros S.A. de C.V.
3ª Cerrada de Minas 501-8, CP 01280 Mexico, D.F.
www.nirvanalibros.com.mx

© Translated from the Spanish by Comunicando Translations & Language Training (Mayte Martín text),
and John King (Mario Vargas Llosa text)
© Translated from the Turkish by: Comunicando Translations & Language Training
© Translated from the Farsi by: Comunicando Translations & Language Training

Style corrections, Carol E. Babylon and Claire Elizabeth Terry

Design: Romi Sanmartí
Typography: Minion 11,2/14,5
Printing and Binding: Índice, Fluvià, 81-87. 08019 Barcelona

First Edition: October 2008
ISBN: 978-84-7245-686-0
Legal deposit: B-32.922/2008

Acknowledgements

Thank you, from the bottom of my heart, to Federico Mayor Zaragoza, President of the Foundation for a Culture of Peace, Josep Samaranch, President of the Friends of UNESCO, Barcelona, and Oleguer Sarsanedas: without your help, support, encouragement and advice, this book would never have seen the light of day.

A special thank you to Agustín Pániker, for all of the above – and your infinite patience!

Thank you also to:

Carol Babylon, for burbling so awfully well; Marianne Berner of Green Cross International for your kindness and help – I'll miss our e-mails! Francesc Rovira, for your help early on & Adriana Tarrés and Isabel Asensio for your help later *on! Sara Barcena, for all your input and support, and a special thank you to www.gatherthewomen.org.*

Thank you to all the staff at Kairós publishers for your graceful professionalism; Karen Holladay, for unwavering support; Gianni Lancellotti, for sentimental reasons; Alicia Farr, for all those names! Bojan Ivic; Aleksandar (Sasa) Kalem; Josefa Casas; Josefina Puche; Rafael Sánchez Barranco; Elaine Withers, for yelling what I needed to hear, when *I needed to hear it! Assumpta Reynal; Norman 'R' Terry; Thubten Wangchen of Tibet House, Barcelona and my son, Roberto, for putting up with me.*

And last, but not least, thank you to all the people who sent in so many kind words of encouragement and support. You don't know how much they meant to me.

Heartfelt thanks for generous practical support for The Art of Living *to:*

Alberto Salgado and Joan Canut, Legal Services/www.salgadoabogados.com
Michelle Burns/www.holistichealingarts.net
Annie Imbens-Fransen/www.uriccs.org/global_council_women
Ankya Klay, Ankya Design One Earth Images/www.ankya.com
Jocelyn Rasmussen/www.morethansinging.com & www.morethanspeaking.com
Rev. Susyn Reeve/www.withforgiveness.com & www.susynreeve.com
Adam Farr, Legal Services
Zahava Sherez, Zahava Sherez Studio/www.zahavasherez.com
Connie Spittler, 'Wise Women Videos'/www.ConnieSpittler.com

Copyrights

Page 21: Used by kind permission of the Office of H.H. The Dalai Lama. From *The Transformed Mind* by the Dalai Lama and Renuka Singh. © 1999 by The Dalai Lama and Renuka Singh. Published by Hodder & Stoughton.

Page 27: Reprinted by kind permission of Edgar Morin. From *Pour une politique de civilisation.* © 1997 by Edgar Morin and Sami Naïr. Published by Arléa, Paris.

Page 33: Reprinted by kind permission of the Office of Prof. Muhammad Yunus. From his Nobel Lecture, December 10th, 2006. © The Nobel Foundation 2006.

Page 39: From *Peace is Every Step* by Thich Nhat Hahn. © 1991 by Thich Nhat Hanh. Used by permission of Bantam Books, a division of Random House, Inc. Published in the UK by Rider and reprinted by permission of The Random House Group Ltd.

Page 55: © Mikhail Gorbachev. Reprinted by kind permission of Green Cross International, from President Gorbachev's article, originally published in Green Cross Optimist Magazine, www.gci.ch.

Page 57: Reprinted by kind permission of Armando Marileo Lefío. © www.mapuche.info.

Page 61: © Wangari Maathai, www.greenbeltmovement.org. Reprinted by kind permission of the Office of Prof. Wangari Maathai. First published in Resurgence, the Magazine of the Heart of Earth, Art and Spirit. www.resurgence.org.

Page 73: Reprinted by kind permission of Refik Algan. © 1992 by Refik Algan. Adapted from *The Dream of the Sleeper,* originally published in Gnosis Magazine, 1992, Issue 22.

Page 79: Reprinted by kind permission of J. Ruth Gendler. From *Notes on the Need for Beauty.* © 2007 by J. Ruth Gendler. Published by Marlowe & Company, an imprint of Avalon Publishing Group, Inc., New York.

Page 81: Reprinted by kind permission of Deepak Chopra. www.deepakchopra.com © Deepak Chopra.

Page 83: From *Leaving Mother Lake* by Yang Erche Namu and Christine Mathieu. © 2003 by Yang Erche Namu and Christine Mathieu. By permission of Little, Brown & Company.

Page 85: Kindly offered for publication in *The Art of Living* by Michael Douglas. From *Newsweek*, September 17th, 2007. © 2007 Newsweek, Inc. All rights reserved. Used by permission and protected by the Copyright Laws of the United States. The printing, copying, redistribution, or retransmission of the Material without express written permission is prohibited.

Page 91: Reprinted by kind permission of the office of Archbishop Desmond Tutu. From *God has a Dream, a Vision of Hope for our Time* by Desmond Tutu and Douglas Abrams. © 2004 by Desmond Tutu. Used by permission of Doubleday, a division of Random House, Inc. Published in the UK by Rider. Reprinted by permission of The Random House Group Ltd.

Page 105: 'Origami', originally part of a longer article, *Origami and the Spiritual*, by David Lister. © David Lister.

Page 107: Reprinted by kind permission of Mario Vargas Llosa. © Mario Vargas Llosa.

Page 121: From an interview by Alan Rusbridger. © Guardian News and Media Ltd 2006.

Page 125: From the forword to *Death and Dying: The Tibetan Tradition*, by Glenn Mullin, Arkana, London,1986.

Page 127: As posted on the Rigpa website (www.rigpaus.org), text adapted from Chapters 1 and 2 from *The Tibetan Book of Living and Dying* by Sogyal Rinpoche and Edited by Patrick Gaffney & Andrew Harvey. © 1993 by Rigpa Fellowship. Reprinted by permission of HarperCollins Publishers. Published in the UK by Rider. Reprinted by permission of The Random House Group Ltd.

Page 133: Reprinted by kind permission of John Berger. From *And our Faces, my Heart, Brief as Photos* by John Berger. © John Berger. Bloomsbury, London, 2005 and Vintage, New York, 1992.

Page 135: Reprinted by kind permission of Prof. Yoel Hoffmann. From *Japanese Death Poems: Written by Zen Monks and Haiku Poets on the Verge of Death*, edited by Yoel Hoffmann. Tuttle Publishing, 1986.

Every effort has been made to ensure that all copyrighted material in this work is correctly credited. In the case of any errors or omissions, please kindly contact the publisher so that the issue may be rectified in future reprints of this work.

In collaboration with:

Amics de la UNESCO de Barcelona

CAIXA CATALUNYA
OBRA SOCIAL

Foundation
Culture of Peace

The profits from this book are being donated to

GREEN CROSS
International

Founded in 1993 by Mikhail Gorbachev, the mission of Green Cross International is to help ensure a just, sustainable and secure future for all by cultivating a new sense of global interdependence and shared responsibility regarding humanity's relationship with nature. GCI has its headquarters in Geneva and National Organizations in 29 countries across five continents. The activities are centered around three main axes:

- Preventing and resolving conflicts over natural resources
- Addressing the environmental consequences of wars and conflicts
- Promoting value and behavior changes

www.greencrossinternational.net

Authors' Websites

Introduction

The Dalai Lama: www.dalailama.com
Federico Mayor Zaragoza: www.fund-culturadepaz.org

Thinking

Edgar Morin: www.iiac.cnrs.fr/cetsah
Candido Mendes: www.candidomendes.br
Muhammad Yunus: www.muhammadyunus.org
Mayte Martín: www.mayte-martin.com

Breathing

Thich Nhat Hanh: www.plumvillage.org
Judith Hurley Prosser: judith4u@att.net
Koichi Barrish: www.tsubakishrine.org

Seeing

Acharya Mahapragya: www.preksha.com
Connie Spittler: www.conniespittler.com
Harvey Lloyd: www.harveylloyd.com

Messages from Mother Earth

Mikhail Gorbachev: www.greencrossinternational.net
Armando Marileo Lefío: www.mapuche.info
Shannon Thunderbird: www.shannonthunderbird.com
Wangari Maathai: www.greenbeltmovement.org
Masaru Emoto: www.hado.net
Debra Landwehr Engle: www.goldentreeco.com

Dreaming

Nofit Itzhak: www.freedom-within.com
Arvick Baghramian: www.freedom-within.com
Refik Algan: www.sufism.org

Love

Oleguer Sarsanedas: www.catradio.cat
J. Ruth Gendler: www.ruthgendler.com
Deepak Chopra: www.deepakchopra.com
Yang Erche Namu: www.namu.com.cn
Michael Douglas: www.un.org/sg/mop/douglas
Pan Guang: www.unaoc.org/content/view/56

Reconciliation

Desmond Tutu: www.tutu.org
Eliyahu McLean: www.jerusalempeacemakers.org
Wayne Kealohi Powell: www.shamanicbodywork.com

Art

Parvin Heydari Nassab: www.shamseh.com
David Lister: www.britishorigami.info/academic/lister
Mario Vargas Llosa: www.mvargasllosa.com

Life

Richard Branson: www.virgin.com
Jean Shinoda Bolen: www.jeanshinodabolen.com
Mehmet Aydin: www.unaoc.org/content/view/34
Ismail Serageldin: www.unaoc.org/content/view/42
Laura Weaver: www.passageworks.org
Alice Herz-Sommer: www.guardian.co.uk/culture

Death

Huston Smith: www.hustonsmith.net
Sogyal Rinpoche: www.rigpa.org
Imam Feisal Abdul Rauf: www.cordobainitiative.org
Gloria Gilmartin: serene8787@yahoo.com
John Berger: www.johnberger.org
Shinsui: www.quietspaces.com/deathpoems.html

In memory, and honour, of all those who lost their lives in the Tsunami of 2004

Foreword

Josep Samaranch, *Spain.*
President, Barcelona Friends of UNESCO.

When Claire Elizabeth Terry first presented the idea for *The Art of Living* to the Barcelona Friends of UNESCO, we realized immediately that it provided a wonderful opportunity to promote those very same values which we espouse. The participation of friends such as Federico Mayor Zaragoza and Agustín Pániker has, finally, turned this idea into a reality.

The Barcelona branch of Friends of UNESCO was born in 1960, thanks to UNESCO itself, which, during the dictatorship, obliged the government of the day to accept its constitution. Since our foundation, we have striven to defend our own language and culture, Catalan, and have become modest defenders of all the world's languages, cultures and ethnic groups.

One of our most successful programs has been *Altaveu per al coneixement i la difusió de les cultures* ('A loudspeaker for the broadcasting of cultural knowledge and awareness'), the aim of which is to recognize the rich heritage of humanity's cultural and linguistic diversity.

For the Barcelona Friends of UNESCO, therefore, Claire's idea has become a priceless opportunity to promote those values which define the 'art of living', as seen by those individuals representative of the world's diverse cultures, religions and perceptions of life. Specifically, it provides a way of highlighting the self-evident reality that life itself is the most important common denominator of all humanity, from which stem all other values, such as human rights, the rights of ethnic groups, and the right to Liberty with a capital L.

The Art of Living is an affirmation of life which helps us reflect on this opportunity which we've been granted. We can only give what we have already, and it is through our appreciation and joy for life itself that we can communicate this optimistic, positive vision to the world around us.

We are convinced that this appreciation for each other should foster and empower a rich sense of solidarity, one of those values of which it has been said, "The more you give, the more you receive."

Solidarity – in all its diverse forms – is something to which we can all contribute, whatever our role, and however we relate to our surroundings.

Barcelona, June 2008

Claire Elizabeth Terry, *England.*
Worked in British theatre as a stage-manager for several years, before becoming a travel writer. She now lives in Barcelona, Spain.

The idea for the *The Art of Living* first came to me after I read Michael (ex-*Monty Python*) Palin's book, *Himalaya*, a few years ago.

Several of his observations, as he journeyed round the lands and cultures within and surrounding the mountains, had the effect of shocking me into the realisation of my own unwitting cultural arrogance. Up until that point in time, like many people, I suppose, I hadn't really given that much thought to the matter of cultural perspective and had just assumed that the culture in which I had grown up had, basically, the right 'take' on the world, and that, as (or so I believed) an open-minded sort of person, it was just necessary to pick a couple of things up from other cultures – to top off the icing on my own particular 'cultural cake', as it were. The more I read, however, the more the thought began to dawn on me: "Claire! It could well be completely the other way round ..."

I remember clearly Oleguer Sarsanedas, one of the people instrumental in getting *The Art of Living* off the ground, saying, in one of our early meetings, "It IS the other way round." I nodded, surprised, but didn't really understand what he meant at the time.

After having had the privilege of editing this book, I do now.

Barcelona, June 2008

Claire Elizabeth Terry

The Art of Living

Contents

Foreword

Introduction

Thinking

Breathing

Seeing

Messages from Mother Earth

Introduction

His Holiness the Dalai Lama, *Tibet.*
His Holiness the 14th Dalai Lama, Tenzin Gyatso,
is the spiritual and temporal leader of the Tibetan people.

We can cultivate and achieve happiness, remove and eliminate suffering, provided we are able to engage in a practice which is in tune with the law of nature and in tune with how things actually exist.

No matter how strong an individual is, we have to live as a human community. If someone lives in isolation, he will eventually experience a lot of mental frustration, because it is human nature to be social. Many of our needs, such as sufficient food and shelter, are provided by the efforts of others. That's the reality, and our daily way of life and thinking should be according to these conditions and factors. Human intelligence is so sophisticated that it sometimes creates an image that hides the reality. Sometimes one is under the false illusion that one is independent and capable of achieving anything, and one does not realize how much one's life is dependent on the existence, help and support of others.

This applies not only to people, but also to the environment and other species; in fact, to everything. A lot of problems and suffering are caused because one is unable to realize the help and support one receives from the surrounding environment, and because one does not pay proper attention and understand their importance.

Even though your focus may be on your personal happiness and well-being, once you are able to understand how much your personal life is dependent on the surrounding environment, you will be able to widen your perspective and your realization of reality. This widened perspective will enable you to create a more harmonious life, not only for yourself but for others as well.

That kind of wider perspective or view then automatically results in a sense of commitment and concern for others. This is not for reasons holy or sacred, but because one's own future depends on these factors.

We have to engage in the practice of non-violence and compassion because of the reality of our interdependence with all other sentient beings.

Federico Mayor Zaragoza, *Spain.*
Professor of Biochemistry. Former Minister of Education and Science, Spain (1981-82) and Director General of UNESCO (1987-99).
President of the Foundation for a Culture of Peace *(Since 2000).*

Sleep and rest just enough to be able to experience intensely the radical mystery of existence.

Thinking

A New Renaissance

Prof. Edgar Morin, *France.*
Philosopher, writer and director of the Centre National de la Recherche Scientifique.

A deterioration in quality for the sake of quantity is the hallmark of our civilisation crisis, since we live in a world dominated by a technological, economic and scientific logic. Only that which is quantifiable is perceived as real, everything else is dismissed, from political thinking in particular. Unfortunately, neither love nor suffering, nor pleasure, enthusiasm or poetry are quantifiable.

Our tools of thought, our ideologies, have proved to be failures: our technological, economic and scientific development, with its specific effects, is a phenomenon unique in history. But borderline situations have occurred in the past. When a given system finds itself saturated with problems it can no longer resolve, it has two possibilities: either general regression or a change of system.

The example of regression is illustrated by that of the Roman Empire. As we know today, it was not the invading hordes that caused the downfall of the Roman Empire, but the fact that Rome proved incapable of changing and of resolving its economic problems. By contrast, the emergence of historic societies in the Middle East some ten thousand years ago, when small nomadic tribes progressed from being hunters and gatherers to taking up agriculture and settling in village communities, is an example of how an overly categorised or dispersed organisational system was successfully overcome to solve the problems posed by a large concentration of populations. Indeed, because globalisation is out of control, it is accompanied by many instances of regression. But it is a possibility that could be desirable.

Obviously, globalisation has a very destructive aspect: it generates anonymity, reduces individual cultures to a common denominator and standardises identities. However, it is also a unique opportunity to promote communication and understanding between the peoples of the planet's various cultures and encourages their blending. This new chapter will come about only once we become fully aware of the fact that we are citizens of the planet first and foremost, and then Europeans, Frenchmen, Africans, Americans ... the planet is our homeland, a fact that does not deny the individual homelands of others. The awareness of our global destiny as a community is the prerequisite for change that would allow us to act as co-pilot for the planet, where our problems have become inextricably intertwined. If not, we would experience a fate similar to that of 'balkanisation', a violent and defensive retaliation against specific ethnic or religious identities, which is the opposite of this process of unification and solidarity throughout the planet.

Pertinent knowledge exists only if one is capable of placing one's information within a context, globalising it and situating it within an overall framework. Our thought system, which permeates education from primary schools to universities, is a system that breaks down reality and renders our minds incapable of linking up the knowledge we are made to pigeonhole into disciplines.

This hyper-specialisation of knowledge, which consists of carving out a single aspect from reality, can have considerable human and practical consequences in the case, for example, of infrastructure policies, which all too often neglect the social and human dimension. It also contributes towards dispossessing citizens of the right to take political decisions and transfers that privilege to experts.

The reforming of thought teaches us to tackle complexity with the aid of concepts capable of re-establishing the links between the different types of knowledge now available to us. Such a reform is crucial in the planetary age where it has become impossible, and artificial, to isolate an important problem at the national level.

This reform of our way of thinking, which itself requires a reforming of education, is not happening anywhere even though it is needed everywhere.

In the 17th century, the philosopher Pascal already understood how everything is linked, realising that "all things aid and are aided, cause and are caused." He even had an understanding of retroaction, which was admirable for his time: "… and everything being linked by an invisible link that binds the parts most distant from one another, I hold it to be impossible to know the parts without knowing the whole, just as it is impossible to know the whole without knowing the parts". That is the crux of the matter, the direction of learning in which education ought to be heading.

But, unfortunately, we have followed the model of Descartes, his contemporary, who for his part advocated breaking down reality and problems into constituent parts. And yet, the whole produces qualities that are not extant in the individual parts. The whole is never just the sum of its parts but always something more. It is essential to be able to consider the unity of the many and the multiplicity of the unit. We tend too much to overlook the unity of mankind when we see the diversity of cultures and customs and to dismiss the diversity when we see the unity. The real problem is being able to see one in the other; after all, the nature of mankind lies precisely in this potential for diversity, which cannot call into question the unity of mankind from an anatomical, genetic, cerebral, intellectual and affective point of view.

It is easy to see, then, that the general and the particular are not conflicting since the general itself is singular. The human race is singular compared with other species yet it produces multiple singularities. Our universe itself is singular yet produces diversity. One must always be able to think of the unit and the multiple; if not, minds incapable of considering the unity of the many and the multiplicity of the unit will inevitably promote a unity that standardises and multiplicities that withdraw into themselves.

I believe we need to open ourselves up to exchange. Just as Asia opened itself up to Western technology, we need to embrace the contributions of Asian, Buddhist and Hindu civilisations in particular, for the part they have played in the relation between oneself and one's inner self, between one's spirit, soul and body, aspects which our productivist and activist civilisation have totally neglected. We have much to learn from other cultures. Just as the Renaissance came about after mediaeval Europe returned to its Greek sources, we now need to find a new Renaissance by drawing from the many sources of the universe.

The Sound of our Times: its silences and overtones

Prof. Candido Mendes, *Brazil.*
Rector of the Universidade Candido Mendes *and Secretary General of the* Académie de la Latinité.

The search for the sound – the tonality – of our times, has become a matter of the utmost urgency, due to the impact of a series of changes worldwide and mankind's attitude towards change itself.

The pervasive syndrome of global fear in recent times, after the fall of the Twin Towers, means that the world's cultures have reached a point of no-return in terms of their co-existence. At the same time, the foundations of our all-embracing modernity are collapsing, as is the Promethean moulding, through technology, of our environment, one that was man-made out of pure self-interest.

Taking as the premise that Western culture has now become *the* universal civilisation, we are, in fact, having to face the expropriation – in all their vital collective identity – of what have become merely peripheral cultures as a result.

A new and very specific 21st century terrorism reflects the emergence of the real 'altericide' – the abolition of the sense of 'otherness' – as the final effect of hegemony, an altericide that extends far beyond the classic recurring patterns of domination and imperialism.

Within this framework, the need to reclaim our cultural diversity is, in fact, essential, if the world is to retain its texture, and be spared from a future that is monotone or deadly silent.

Just as innovation became the benchmark for the modern age, so cultural diversity should be the imperative for the future, one that is as global as it is intrinsically pluralistic.

Reconfiguring the World

Dr. Muhammad Yunus, *Bangladesh.*
Founder, Grameen Bank, *(co-recipients of the Nobel Peace Prize), which provides microcredit to entrepreneurs in rural Bangladesh who have no collateral.*

We get what we want, or what we don't refuse. We accept the fact that we will always have poor people around us, and that poverty is part of human destiny. This is precisely why we continue to have poor people around us. If we firmly believed that poverty was unacceptable to us, and that it should not belong to a civilized society, we would have built appropriate institutions and policies to create a poverty-free world.

We wanted to go to the moon, so we went there. We achieve what we want to achieve. If we are not achieving something, it is because we have not put our minds to it. We create what we want.

What we want and how we get to it depends on our mindsets. It is extremely difficult to change mindsets once they are formed. We create the world in accordance with our mindset. We need to invent ways to change our perspective continually and reconfigure our mindset quickly as new knowledge emerges. We can reconfigure our world, if we can reconfigure our mindset.

I believe that we can create a poverty-free world because poverty is not created by poor people. It has been created and sustained by the economic and social system that we have designed for ourselves; the institutions and concepts that make up that system; the policies that we pursue.

Poverty is created because we built our theoretical framework on assumptions which underestimate human capacity, by designing concepts which are too narrow (such as concepts of business, credit-worthiness, entrepreneurship, employment) or by developing institutions which remain half-completed (such as financial institutions, where the poor are left out). Poverty is caused by failure at the conceptual level, rather than any lack of capability on the part of people.

I firmly believe that we can create a poverty-free world if we collectively believe in it. In a poverty-free world, the only place you would be able to see poverty would be in poverty museums. When schoolchildren took a tour of the poverty museums, they would be horrified to see the misery and indignity that some human beings had had to go through. They would blame their forefathers for having tolerated this inhumane condition, which existed for so long, for so many people.

A human being is born into this world fully equipped, not only to take care of him- or herself, but also to contribute to enlarging the well-being of the world as a whole. Some get the chance to explore their potential to some degree, but many others never get any opportunity during their lifetime to unwrap the wonderful gift they were born with. They die unexplored and the world remains deprived of their creativity, and their contribution.

Grameen Bank has given me an unshakable faith in the creativity of human beings. This has led me to believe that human beings are not born to suffer the misery of hunger and poverty.

To me, poor people are like bonsai trees. When you plant the best seed of the tallest tree in a flowerpot, you get a replica of the tallest tree, only inches tall. There is nothing wrong with the seed you planted, only the soil-base that is too inadequate. Poor people are bonsai people. There is nothing wrong with their seeds. Simply, society never gave them the base on which to grow. All it needs to get poor people out of poverty is for an enabling environment to be created for them. Once the poor can unleash their energy and creativity, poverty will disappear very quickly.

the time of nothingness

Mayte Martín, *Spain.*
Flamenco singer. Renowned for her elegance, versatility and artistic honesty, she embodies a highly individualistic and rebellious philosophy within the world of flamenco.

there is only one stave on which we can write the symphony of our own life. one pencil with which to outline the map which alone, and then only sometimes, can cheat destiny. the clay with which to mould that which we don't want, in order never to forget what it looks like:
the time of nothingness.

i know very little about many things. i've dedicated the majority of my life to learning from myself, through those reactions which created a sense of alienation in me: through what i heard, what i saw ... i dedicated time to this which i 'should' have used to learn about which were the highest mountains in the world, or which river bathed which land. you could say that i dedicated too much time, if it weren't for the fact that time has its own dimensions, unalterable, and we only become aware of the true treasure contained within it when we have a clear understanding of how we'd like to fill it. and to discover this, we need it to be empty, transparent, neutral: the time of nothingness.

music is the vehicle which i use to express my way of seeing life, my idea of freedom; to champion the logic of my soul. and there is something fundamental in my life, and which i consider to be fundamental in the lives of all human beings, because it's absolutely essential to be aware of what this logic is: the time of nothingness.

i am not afraid of being wrong, because my mistakes always come from a freely contemplated decision. those mistakes which are freely-made are welcome. i am only afraid of inertia. of not spending time taking decisions. of not giving myself time to discover that i must take them. that time passes and they take me.

my greatest fear would be that things formed part of my life against my choice and wishes, because i would never have been aware that i didn't want them. there is only one thing that my happiness and freedom could never renounce, because without it they would not exist: the time of nothingness.

Editor's note: The absence of capitals in this text is according to the author's wishes.

Breathing

Conscious Breathing

Thich Nhat Hanh, *Vietnam.*
Zen Master and Buddhist monk. Founder of Plum Village Buddhist Community *in France.*

Every morning, when we wake up, we have twenty-four brand-new hours to live. What a precious gift! We have the capacity to live in a way that these twenty-four hours will bring peace, joy, and happiness to ourselves and others.

Peace is present right here and now, in ourselves and in everything we do and see. The question is whether or not we are in touch with it. We don't have to travel far away to enjoy the blue sky. We don't have to leave our city or even our neighborhood to enjoy the eyes of a beautiful child. Even the air we breathe can be a source of joy.

We can smile, breathe, walk, and eat our meals in a way that allows us to be in touch with the abundance of happiness that is available. We are very good at preparing to live, but not very good at living. We know how to sacrifice ten years for a diploma, and we are willing to work very hard to get a job, a car, a house, and so on. But we have difficulty remembering that we are alive in the present moment, the only moment there is for us to be alive. Every breath we take, every step we make, can be filled with peace, joy, and serenity. We need only to be awake, alive in the present moment.

A simple technique is, that as we breathe in, we say to ourselves, "Breathing in, I know that I am breathing in." And as we breathe out, we say, "Breathing out, I know that I am breathing out."

Just that. We recognize our in-breath as an in-breath and our out-breath as an out-breath. This technique can help us keep our minds on our breath. As we practise, our breath will become peaceful and gentle, and our minds and bodies will also become peaceful and gentle. In just a few minutes we can realize the fruits of meditation.

Breathing in and out is very important, and it is enjoyable. Our breathing is the link between our body and our mind. Sometimes our mind is thinking of one thing and our body is doing another, and mind and body are not unified. By concentrating on our breathing, "In" and "Out," we bring body and mind back together, and become whole again. Conscious breathing is an important bridge.

To me, breathing is a joy that I cannot miss. Every day, I practise conscious breathing, and in my small meditation room, I have calligraphed this sentence: "Breathe, you are alive!" Just breathing and smiling can make us very happy, because when we breathe consciously we recover ourselves completely and encounter life in the present moment.

Breathe

Judith Hurley Prosser, *USA.*

An artist who began writing poetry in 2002 as part of her meditation practice, she lives with her husband in the Sierra Foothills of Northern California.

Breathe in.
Breathe out.
Breathe in,
Draw up Earth's Energy
Into your body.
Breathe out,
Pull down Universal Light
Into your body.
Breathe in,
Be grounded
In your body.
Breathe out,
Allow wisdom to
Fill your Being.
Breathe in
Life itself.
Breathe out
All things unnecessary.
Breathe in.
Breathe out.

The Sun

Rev. Koichi Barrish, *USA.*
Senior Shinto priest, Tsubaki Grand Shrine of America, *Washington State.*

Ueshiba Morihei O'Sensei, the great Shinto thinker and founder of the Art of Aikido said:

"Rise early in the morning to greet the Sun. Inhale and let yourself soar to the ends of the Universe; breath out and let the Cosmos inside. Next, breath up the fecundity and vibrance of Earth. Blend the breath of Earth and your own and become the breath of life itself. Your mind and body will be gladdened, depression and heartache will dissipate and you will be filled with light and gratitude."

The basis of Shinto thinking is that all things on Earth, including human beings, receive their lives from *Taiyo*, the Sun, or solar progenitor.

The word for 'human being' in Japanese is *hito*. The ancient way of defining this word is as 'a temporary repository for divine solar energy' and the Shinto way of viewing our human lives is as divided cells of this same energy.

Of course, this thinking appears rather simple and primitive when we first consider it – however, if we examine it more deeply, we can see that it has a scientific basis, as all the material of our bodies was present at the origin of the solar system. Solar power is stored in the food we eat, so when we chew we can release this energy to power our cells and sustain our own lives.

To realize this is to come into accord with life and instantly understand all our relationships. To realize this is to be filled with joy and deep gratitude for the great gifts of life, received through the Sun, Divine Beings and Ancestors and sustained by Great Nature and our Human Family.

If we can remember where we come from, then we know we are interconnected as beams of light refracted through one great prism.

Seeing

Darsha

Acharya Mahapragya, *India.*
Jain monk, spiritual head and discoverer of Preksha *meditation.*

Indian philosophy, or '*darsha*', is based on perception, or seeing. In fact, '*darsha*' *means* seeing or perceiving. Its meaning has changed now. The philosophy being taught in colleges and universities today is based on inference and reasoning, but in ancient times it stood for direct apprehension. Not inference, not abstract reasoning, not causation, not universality or pervasiveness, but sheer apprehension. Today, we have lost the power to see and we fail to distinguish between thinking and perceiving.

To illustrate: once a philosopher and his friend were walking together. They saw a cow and its owner coming from the opposite direction. The cow was tied with a rope, one end of which the owner held in his hand. The philosopher saw the whole situation and apprehended.

He asked his friend to tell him whether the cow was tied to the man or the man to the cow. The latter thought that it was too simple a matter to need any serious thought; since it was the man who held the rope in his hand, it was the cow that was bound.

Then the philosopher asked him what the man would do if the cow broke loose and fled. Pat came the reply: he would run after the cow and catch it. If that was true, the philosopher said, it was clear who was tied to whom. If the man ran away, the cow would not run after him, but if the cow ran away the man would have to run after it.

Superficial thinking would suggest the cow was tied to the man, but Indian philosophy would suggest the owner was tied to the cow, for it implies direct apprehension and 'seeing' in the sense of perceiving.

Perceiving, then, is a very important aspect of being alive: we also need to be able to perceive our breath, as well as our whole body and its psychic centres. One might ask: what is there, in breath, for example, to see? We breathe in and out and this goes on for as long as we live. So what is so special about it which merits seeing? The answer is, that through seeing or perceiving the breath we come to recognise its immense worth, for seeing the breath, or 'breath perception', is the best way to control our thoughts and so steady the wanderings of our minds.

Lint

Connie Spittler, *Sonara Desert, USA.*
Essayist and poet; wrote & produced the Wise Women *videos, selected for Harvard University's Library on the History of Women in America.*

Years ago, I met a man who noticed lint. After Reinhold Marxhausen watched his wife clean the clothes dryer screen, he began to collect this peculiar stuff, not seeing throwaway material, but texture, color and invention. A Professor of Art at Concordia College in Nebraska, he layered the multi-colored fibers under glass, forming abstractions that echoed landscape. I bought one, as a reminder to look more closely at my immediate world.

'The philosophy of lint', I call it, a way of noticing beauty in the simplest of things, which was Marxhausen's intention all along. Value the commonplace, he meant. See the abstract cracks in the asphalt. Appreciate the symmetry of dead branches and the last soap bubble in the tub. Watch the pattern of light and shadow playing on the wall.

It was this way of living that made my husband and I notice the passage of light in the kitchen, as I cooked supper in the afternoon. The sun journeys through the paned window, rays casting lingering patterns on old lace cloth or red paisley runner. We watch arms of the sun catch swirls in green glass plates that belonged to my husband's mother or wash over the oriental designs of chipped blue and white china. Fading brilliance turns the copper bowl of yellow coyote gourds from the nearby wash into a Renaissance still life. The effect of sunshine on our table remains remarkable. Transitory. Free.

It took a while, but eventually we noticed the spear of light that began to move through the kitchen to the next room. The more we watched the daily shift of sun, the more intrigued we became. Months later, we discovered that twice a year this piercing light traveled through the kitchen, the next room and down the long hall leading to the bedrooms, coming to rest on the linen closet door. With hints of Stonehenge on Equinox, we reveled in time's transitions marked in the heart of our house by an intense, narrow beam. Was it planned? Over thirty years ago, did the builder envision this phenomenon before or during construction? Unlikely, but we wondered if other occupants had seen the seasonal ray that split the late afternoon air, seeking the depths of a dark and narrow hallway? We'll never know. But we see it. The sun in its cycle announces either that Summer will soon be over or Spring is on the way, in celebration of the art of noticing, my 'philosophy of lint'.

Light is God

Harvey Lloyd, *New York City, USA.*
Artist, photojournalist and writer. Has spent over 40 years and traveled more than a million-and-a-half miles witnessing and recording life on Earth through his lens.

Our eyes do not see, any more than our computer thinks. Our eyes are marvelous tools for recording and transmitting photons of light to our brains in the form of electrical signals. Beginning at the retina, a series of computer-like programs analyze, censor, delete and send certain amounts of information to various parts of the brain. This is not widely understood. Most of us were raised and taught that we 'see' with our eyes.

Recent studies of how the eye and brain work together bring to light the uncanny fact that it is our brains, and not our eyes, which 'see' and control our vision and that it is our early conditioning and genetic inheritance which determine *how* and *what* we see.

Wordsworth, in his poem, 'Intimations of Immortality from Recollections of Early Childhood' wrote:

"There was a time when meadow, grove, and stream,
The earth, and every common sight,
To me did seem
Appareled in celestial light,
The glory and the freshness of a dream.
It is not now as it hath been of yore;
Turn wheresoe'er I may,
By night or day,
The things which I have seen I now can see no more."

"The human mind is not capable of grasping the universe. We are like a little child entering a huge library. The walls are covered from floor to ceiling with books in many different tongues. The child knows that someone must have written these books. It does not know who or how. It does not understand the languages in which they are written. But the child notes a definite plan in the arrangement of the books ... a mysterious order which it doesn't comprehend, but only dimly suspects." *

Each of us is that happy child for whom all of creation, from the earth to the starry universe, awaits recognition.

Einstein's Theory of Relativity revealed a new world in which the speed of light could not be surpassed, and where time was not a universal clock – his concept of the space-time continuum. He saw into the hidden workings of the universe. Each of us, genius or not, is capable of seeing beyond the veil of self-imposed or peer-imposed 'reality.'

Firstly, we need to understand that our eyes are as miraculous, or even more so, than the Hubble Space Telescope. They are not windows. Our open eyes gather quintillions of photons every minute. Such a myriad of riches must be organized. Our eyes and our brains have been marvelously trained by evolution to do just this. They are trained to work at our daily tasks, but not to reveal the hidden world around us.

We see everything, but we hide most of what we see behind a veil in order to avoid being overwhelmed.

It's necessary to be overwhelmed now and then, to penetrate the veil, like a deep-sea diver overcoming his initial fear of drowning. Underwater photographic techniques have revealed the astonishing rainbows of wonders beneath the surface of the sea to eyes and brains that had no preconditioning, and therefore censored nothing. We glory in these wondrous visions, while all around us, on Terra Firma, a thousand visions go unnoticed.

Let's dive deep into the 'sea' on firm land and begin to see as children once again.

* Albert Einstein.

Messages from Mother Earth

A new *Glasnost* for the Planet

Mikhail Gorbachev, *Russia.*
Former President of the Soviet Union and Founding President of Green Cross International.

It may seem paradoxical, but despite having borne witness to the countless humanitarian and environmental disasters of recent decades, I am an optimist.

But being an optimist does not mean simply looking at the world through rose-tinted glasses, like Voltaire's Candide, and declaring everything to be for the best, despite an endless array of misfortunes. Being an optimist, as I see it, means to refuse to make do with the status quo, and instead to consciously look for ways to make the world a better place and help address the practical challenges faced by people here and now.

I call this 'optimism by action', and I believe that such a philosophy of life can provide the catalyst for our much-needed transformation to sustainable development.

Twenty years ago, when *Glasnost* – openness – was used to launch the process of *Perestroika* that transformed the Soviet Union, no one believed that it was doable. But I was driven by the need to 'wake up' those people who had 'fallen asleep' and make them truly active and concerned; to ensure that everyone felt as if they were master of their country, of their enterprise, office or institute: to fully involve the individual in all of the processes concerned.

Today, I am convinced that, as citizens of the world, we need a reformulated *Glasnost* to invigorate, inform and inspire us to put the staggering resources of our planet and our knowledge of it, to use for the benefit of all of Earth's citizens.

Glasnost could be put to service as a catchall phrase for all of the instruments in the struggle for transparency and awareness. *Glasnost* is more than transparency; it is a demanding, long-term process of awakening which inevitably leads to calls for fundamental changes. A reversal of currently prevalent behavioral patterns must begin with changes in the human spirit and a reprioritization of our value system, including relationships between people, and the man-nature interrelationship.

This means solidarity of a higher order than that of previous models found in small groups, communities and social movements: one that more equitably balances the burdens and benefits of globalization and brings about a just and caring world order. It is a solidarity that presents itself as the pillar of sustainable development in all its human and inter-generational aspects.

"Judge not by words, but by deeds," should be our mantra. This is precisely why we need a new *Glasnost* for the planet, one that will inspire its citizens to become actively involved today in the struggle for a better tomorrow.

I believe in people and will remain an optimist – an active one – calling for dynamic and positive change.

Mapudungun: The Earth Is Speaking

Armando Marileo Lefío, *Chile.*
The Ngenpin, *Ancestral Spiritual Authority for the Mapuche Community in Lake Budi, and founder of the* Mapuche Ancestral School of Philosophy and Wisdom *in Temuco, Chile.*

One of the most important achievements of our ancestors was the development of a communication system wholly reliant on the languages of the earth and nature, that is, natural codes, sounds, messages and means of communication.

In the cycle of the seasons or stages of the year, messages are constantly being delivered by birds, rivers, the rain and wind, leaves, and insects such as crickets. These messages can guide our actions, to the extent to which we are able to decode them. Otherwise we remain puzzled.

If our ancestors had not managed to understand such messages from nature, they might not have been able to determine our role in nature, our reason for being and our destiny. Fortunately, they realised the fundamental importance of understanding the messages from the earth and nature, so that by deciphering the sounds of rivers, the whistling of the wind, the howling of the sea, the singing of birds, the sounds of leaves, insects and animals, the Mapudungun – the Mapuche language – was created: the "speech of the earth", a very specific way of communicating.

Our grandparents used to say, "The universe as a whole, the whole of nature and the earth is an open book. They guide us, help us to foresee danger, and teach us. All that is required to receive that message is to pay attention and to open up our hearts."

Birdsong has a specific melody or sound depending on its intended message.

At dawn, mists or reddish clouds determine the day's weather. Mists waving over the mountains like smoke coming out of a ruka, *or house, indicate that the spirits of nature are beginning their daily activity.*

The noise of the sea, the direction of the wind, the flight of seagulls or the angle of the moon can enable us to determine with great precision the day and even the time of the coming rain. The blossoming of the quilas* *announces a big event, maybe a famine or a war.*

* The Mapuche name for a bush in Chile which never flowers nor bears fruit, except to augur disaster.

The position of the moon at certain times of the year tells us which economic activities should be pursued and when: sowing, castrating, ear piercing, logging or even traveling into another dimension through the 'Door of Time'.

Everything has a message which can be deciphered, depending on the time of year and our desire to learn from nature's mysteries and challenges.

Decoded by our ancestors, such messages enabled them to create a means of communication called the Mapudungun, which belongs to the land and not to us, because it wasn't we who created its sounds but nature itself.

Noo Halidzoks

Shannon Thunderbird, *Canada.*
Gisbutwada Clan of the Coast Tsimshian Indigenous People.
Speaker, traditional teacher and singer-songwriter, celebrating 'Turtle Island's' Indigenous Peoples.

At the root of all Native teachings lies a reverence for The Land. *Noo Halidzoks*, or Mother Earth, gave the Red People a special gift of Turtle Island, or North America. We were charged with the responsibility of being caretakers of this vast Land and were given much wisdom and knowledge with regard to its care and preservation. As an Elder once said, "We are the environment and the environment is us. We deal with all of nature as equal members of the Universal Family. We go to the mountain, we go into the mountain, we become the mountain – never trying to overcome it, but always being part of its energy."

There was a fundamental misunderstanding in the early dialogues between First Nations Peoples and the Europeans who sought to purchase our Land. My ancestors were mystified by such negotiations, because The Land was not something to be bought and sold. The Land was the lifeblood of The People: its inherent sacredness lived in the souls of every member of the Red Race. It was to be kept in a good way, nourished and loved. In the words of Chief Sealth (also known as 'Seattle'), "How can I sell what I do not own? It is only owned by that which created it in the first place." The rest, as is said, is history, as The Land was then simply taken from the First Peoples, and quickly became a marketable commodity by which great riches could be gained, regardless of the global devastation that ensued.

As human beings, we need to look around, and into our hearts and learn from this. Balance and harmony were built into the original world and it was never the intention of *Noo Halidzoks* for The Land to have no meaning except for financial profit.

We need to embrace *Noo Halidzoks*, our Mother Earth, with pureness, dignity, peace and constructive energy so that together we can save what is left of her. When we 'Walk the Earth Walk' with the twin elements of knowledge and courage – the knowledge of the importance of The Land to our living world, and the courage to save it – all things will be possible. All My Relations.*

* *Editor's note:* For indigenous peoples, 'All My Relations' signifies, 'All my relationships whith all living beings.'

The Cracked Mirror

Prof. Wangari Maathai, *Kenya.*
Founder of The Green Belt Movement *& Nobel Peace Prize Winner.*

Mount Kenya used to be a holy mountain for my people, the Kikuyus. They believed that their God dwelled on the mountain and that everything good – the rains and clean drinking water – flowed from it. As long as they saw the clouds (the mountain is a very shy mountain, usually hiding behind clouds), they knew they would get rain.

And then the missionaries came. With all due respect to the missionaries – they are the ones who really taught me – in their wisdom, or lack of it, they said, "God does not dwell on Mount Kenya. God dwells in heaven."

We have been looking for heaven, but we haven't found it. Men and women have gone to the moon and back and have not seen heaven. Heaven is not above us: it is right here, right now. So the Kikuyu people were not wrong when they said that God dwelled on the mountain, because if God is omnipresent, as theology teaches us, then God is on Mount Kenya too. If believing that God is on Mount Kenya is what helps people conserve their mountain, I say that's okay. If people still believed this, they would not have allowed illegal logging or clear-cutting of the forests.

After working with different Kenyan communities for more than two decades, the Green Belt Movement which I founded in 1977 also concluded that culture should be incorporated into any development paradigm that has at its heart the welfare of the people. We realised that some of the communities had lost aspects of their culture which had actually facilitated the conservation of that beautiful environment which the first European explorers and missionaries recorded in their diaries and textbooks.

Culture is an important part of humanity. Too often, when we talk about conservation, we don't think about culture. But we human beings have evolved in the environment in which we find ourselves. For every one of us, wherever we were, the environment shaped us: it shaped our values; it shaped our bodies; it shaped our religion. It really defined who we are and how we see ourselves.

By the end of the civic and environmental seminars organised by the Green Belt Movement, participants feel the time has come for them to hold up their own mirror and find out who they are. This is why we call the seminars *kwimenya* (self-knowledge). Until then, participants have looked through someone else's mirror – the mirror of the missionaries or their teachers or the colonial authorities who have told them who they are and who write and speak about them – at their own cracked reflections. They have seen only a distorted image, if they have seen themselves at all!

A new attitude toward nature provides space for a new attitude toward culture and the role it plays in sustainable development: an attitude based on a new understanding – that self-identity, self-respect, morality, and spirituality play a major role in the life of a community and its capacity to take steps that benefit it and ensure its survival.

Of course, no one culture is applicable to all human beings who wish to retain their self-respect and dignity; none can satisfy all communities. Humanity needs to find beauty in its diversity of cultures and accept that there will be many languages, religions, attires, dances, songs, symbols, festivals and traditions. This diversity should be seen as a Universal Heritage of Humankind.

Only when communities recapture those positive aspects of their culture which have been eroded through colonialism or other factors, will people re-learn how to love themselves and what is theirs. Only then will they really appreciate their country and the need to protect its natural beauty and wealth. And only then will they have a true understanding of the future and the generations to come.

Homage to Water
A Song to Praise You

Dr. Masaru Emoto, *Japan.*
Discovered that crystals formed in frozen water reveal changes when specific thoughts are directed towards them. Author of The Hidden Messages in Water.

You are the one who continues to give the energy of life so generously to all animals and plants. Thank you.

You are the one who nourishes heaven and earth, the one who creates oceans, lakes, and rivers, the one who creates all life. Thank you.

Sometimes you hold your energy by becoming ice, hard and cold, sometimes releasing it by dancing in the sky as mist or cloud, and sometimes you permeate the soil by becoming rain or snow, healing our Gaia. A broad and magnanimous heart, like God. Thank you.

Without you the world is dark and nothing can exist. So as humans on behalf of nature and all living things, we should always express to you our love, gratitude and respect. Until now we have neglected you and taken you for granted, without realizing how great your existence is to us. But through water crystals I came to know that you have the same heart as ours. Yes, you are the mirror of our heart. If we become consumed by greed so too do you, swallowing everything.

We are sorry for what has been happening till now. We vow to you that we will love, thank and respect you always.

The Land

Debra Landwehr Engle, *USA.*
Writer and teacher, she lives in Madison County, Iowa, with her husband Bob and dog Wolf.

I live in Madison County, Iowa, home of the covered bridges for which a book and movie were named. *The Bridges of Madison County* spoke of unrequited love, heartbreak, and longing, all the emotions in Clint Eastwood's face at the end of the movie as he stood in the rain and watched his love drive away.

But I can tell you that love lives on in Madison County. In fact, my husband and I married here five years ago, creating an altar between a small pine and Russian olive tree in our back yard. We set up hay bales as seats for our guests and decorated the yard with potted mums and prayer flags that swayed from branches and fenceposts. Our neighbor's cows came to pasture at the back of our yard that day, and just before sunset, the last rays of the sun streamed across the hills and through the trees, casting a golden light over everyone at the ceremony.

Now, five years later, I am reminded daily of the connection between romance and the land. It's true romance - the love of a higher power, of ourselves and one another.

When we moved to this house, I stretched out on the ground one day with my arms spread out to my sides, soaking up the earth energy. In my mind, I saw an entire tribal nation of Indians, as though my elders were teaching me respect for these rolling hills. Since that day, they have shown me the change in the sky as thunderstorms roll in. I've paid attention when the grasshoppers come, and the butterflies, and the bluebirds. I've learned when the land will be cool and when it will be warm. I've watched plants find renewal in rain, marked the growing cycles of corn, and stood in wonder at a field of soybeans waving in the wind like a length of velvet.

There are hills in this landscape, yes. And also flat places and low places and water and weeds and brilliant flowers that you plant and wildflowers that plant themselves. It is sacred ground, a land of enchantment, an answer to prayer.

Romance isn't only in the covered bridges, in Clint Eastwood's haggard face in the rain. It is in us, in the art of loving the earth on which we stand.

Dreaming

Subtle Letters

Nofit Itzhak, *Israel.*
Training as a therapist and currently studying towards a Ph.D in Psychological Anthropology.

During the first month of my mother's pregnancy and while she was still unaware that she was with child, my grandmother dreamt of her late husband. In her dream, my grandfather appeared and gave her a baby girl. He explained to whom the baby belonged, then gave her the bundled infant and left. When she woke up the following morning, she came to my mother, her sixth daughter, and told her, "You are about to give birth to your first daughter". Although throughout her pregnancy both family members and friends insisted that my mother would give birth to a boy, my grandmother wouldn't budge. "It's a girl", she said. And she was right, of course.

Growing up with this story, as a child I was taught never to doubt the power and wisdom of dreams. Dreams were not only prophetic, they were also the means by which the souls of the dead communicated with us; they were the gateway between this world and the next one.

Jewish people from all over the world pay special attention to dreams concerning the dead. In fact, all of the 'lessons' I have received about dream interpretation from my grandmother and mother referred to visits from the spirits of deceased relatives.

To my surprise, I found later on in life, that similar ideas regarding dream interpretation were shared by Jewish people of vastly different cultures. I was taught by my Persian Jewish grandmother that a dead person appearing in a dream and eating was a warning of a possible misfortune or even death in the family. I was also warned that if ever I dreamt of a dead person asking for food, I was to refuse them and send them away. Many years after first having learnt this, I came across a Moroccan Jewish woman who expressed this very same idea. As I grew older, the lessons I first learned about dreams have stayed with me, to be joined by many others.

More than anything, I have come to understand how my dreams could wake me up to truths about myself that I had previously been unaware of. I have come to recognize that truly, as the Jewish proverb says, "A dream not interpreted is like a letter unread", and those times when I do manage to read and understand these subtle letters sent to me, I am able to uncover invaluable treasures.

Shamanic Dreaming

Arvick Baghramian, *Iran.*
Armenian Shamanic counselor, psychotherapist, and author of The Magic of Shamanism.

I was brought up in a culture where people valued their dreams, and their lives were guided by them. They would look to their dreams in search of answers and would take the trouble of having their dreams interpreted for them whenever a particular dream struck them as especially significant.

Whenever a person of my Armenian community in Iran was worried, sick or distressed, they would come to my mother and ask her to 'dream for them' in search for an answer to their problems. Dreams were understood, through interpreting the symbols appearing in them, and the belief in their importance is so strong among Armenians, that at the end of Armenian calendars a special section is dedicated to specify the meaning assigned to countless possible dream symbols.

It is, therefore, common knowledge that if someone dreams of shoes, for example, they should expect to travel in the near future – or alternately to receive a great sum of money; while if they dream of earrings they should expect to suffer the disappointment of an unfulfilled expectation.

However, even as a child, I was not really at ease with this notion of assigning set meanings to symbols. As I grew older and chose to become a psychotherapist, my childhood doubts were confirmed and it became clear to me that the art of dream interpretation involved more than simply assigning prescribed meanings to symbols. I realized that, just as each person was unique, so were the meanings of the symbols appearing in their dreams, and that these symbols had to be interpreted according to the complex circumstances of the dreamer's own life and in accordance with the dreamer's own personal understanding of the symbols.

As my life path brought me to practice shamanism, my understanding of dreams and their roles in our lives deepened even further. As my spirit teacher, or guide, once told me on a shamanic journey, "Dreams come from your innocent soul, from the pure aspect of yourself, to teach you and to wake you up to who you really are. Your dreams will direct you on your path, if you take notice of them. The spirits talk to you through your dreams. Listen to them."

People of shamanic cultures from all over the Earth believe that there exists a world parallel to our ordinary material one. This is the world of the spirits, and it is to this invisible world that the community's shaman journeys, to bring back with her the wisdom and power of the spirit teachers.

Many shamans consider the spirit world to be the true world, our ordinary reality being nothing but an illusion or a 'lie'. Access to this spirit world is gained through an alteration of the shaman's state of consciousness, but according to most shamanic cultures, we have all visited the spirit world countless times. Every night as we go to sleep, our soul flies away to the realms of the spirits. We dream.

The Polished Mirror

Refik Algan, *Turkey.*
Originally studied medicine and worked as a medical consultant.
He is now a Sufi teacher, writer and translator of mystical Turkish classical literature.

Are all dream systems relativistic, or can there be a single, absolute dream system in which no symbolism is presumed?

One of the main characteristics of an operating dream system, even if it be mostly relativistic, is its accordance with the function and structure of the brain itself. Therefore, even a relativistic dream system (such as that of a particular Sufi order) sooner or later has to pass from relativistic imagery to certain points of contact with the objective world, and finally, one has to end at an absolute destination, which is the brain's naked structure itself, i.e. the 'hardware'. At a certain stage dreams will begin to reflect certain objective features of the nervous system. As the Turkish poet Yunus Emre said, "We found it all in the body."

These points of contact with the objective world are closely related to the problems of objectivity, free will, and predestination. On the other hand, although there may be an absolute dream system beyond relativistic approaches, the seeker's own previous psychological structure translates this into his or her own relativistic system, and this goes on until the absolute and objective features begin to dominate.

Although dreams are not the only criteria, the frequency of the appearance of absolute themes (that is, those relating to the divine) within the seeker's dreams indicates the degree of his or her closeness to the objective world. Here is where the interval between the subjective and objective begins to diminish. At last, being freed from relativistic and personal dreams, the brain can see the outside world as it is. Then the inside and outside have become one and there is no veil of ignorance between them.

From then on, as has been traditionally expressed, "The mirror has been polished" or cleaned of dreams. In modern terms, one has reached objective consciousness. This is the state where the outside is reflected onto the inside without distortion.

Do dreams come to an end here? Is there also a symbolism, perhaps even an absolute one, for the objective world?

On the one hand, the outward world and its events may be grossly distorted by our subjectivity. As we undergo the process of cleaning the mirror of the heart, we move from subjectivity to objectivity. We free ourselves from the gross distortions of our egoism. Eventually we may begin to approach the seeing of that Divine Interpreter to whom the real meaning of all things is clear.

As Muhammad said, "The world is like a dream that a sleeping man sees."

Love

Why we are here

Oleguer Sarsanedas, *Spain.*
Born in Glasgow. Has worked in the fields of media and communications all his life and is currently the Managing Director of Catalunya Ràdio, *Barcelona, Spain.*

The art of living, like the art of loving, is about listening to one's soul – that is, one's heart and conscience. This is why we are here.

In the Field of Love

J. Ruth Gendler, *USA*.
Artist, writer and teacher, she has been interested in the intersection of art and writing, language and vision, since a child and is the author of The Book of Qualities.

When we are most alive, we are beautiful. When we are in love, we are reminded that we are beautiful. And sometimes when we know we are beautiful, we find ourselves in love.

'In love' usually means the romantic sense of being with another person who in that moment we feel reflects us perfectly. In love, living in the field of love.

Sometimes I have felt like I was in love, even when there was no one I was in love with. I couldn't talk about my lover's hands or eyes or voice. I couldn't focus all this love on one other, and it was both confusing and revealing to realize how much we become places for each other to rest in.

Alone and 'in love', it's easy to feel like you're making it up. Our songs and our movies have told us such great sentimental stories about being 'in love', that we forget that being in love can be a state of truth as well as an illusion.

Longtime friends witnessing a friend 'falling in love' often caution the infatuated person that being in love is a dizzy, temporary state. I prefer to think of this territory not just as a delicious romantic dance, but as a field to which we can travel from many places. There is a way in which being in love with anything – a person, a place, a project – is crossing a border into a country where the ego does not rule, into a state of being where essence is honored.

We are both inside and outside our everyday selves.

I never want to underestimate the capacity that being 'in love' has to change our seeing, to expand our vision, and to remind us of both human beauty and human frailty.

The search for the beloved is full of paradoxes. We want to be who we are when we are our best self, and sometimes because we have met that self when we are in love, we believe that self only exists in the presence of the other. So we hold on to the other and lose ourselves, forgetting that love is partly of this world and partly of some other place.

An old beau once spoke to me of the danger of trying to make our lovers be God, insisting that we each need our own relationship to the Source. It sounded logical, but I rebelled at his analysis. In this world, one of the ways we glimpse God is when we are in love. Not that the beloved is God, but that God is the Beloved, a tradition as old as the Song of Songs and the ecstatic poems of wandering Indian mystics, the Sufis.

One of the most beautiful and accessible ways to address God is as Love.

The Greeks gave us an image of Eros, the unpredictable archer before whom even the Gods trembled. Hindus tell their stories of the Gopi maidens seeking Krishna, the bewitchingly beautiful, blue-skinned god; Krishna with his soft glowing eyes and perfumed hair, Krishna drawing women to him, touching in each forgotten registers of being.

What is done with love, is done in beauty to celebrate the God who loves.

More and more I believe in the messengers of love, the envoys and the couriers of beauty who are everywhere.

And I wonder how something so clear can also be so mysterious.

Intimacy

Deepak Chopra, *India.*
www.deepakchopra.com

The Latin word *intimus*, from which we get the word intimacy, means 'the innermost.' So intimacy is the experience of allowing our innermost self to be touched by the world, to be moved, to be transformed. Ecstasy is the experience of total intimacy – with God, with nature, with life, with the universe – but above all, with ourselves.

We can only be intimate with others to the extent that we can be intimate with ourselves. We need to be fully present to our own pain, our vulnerability and broken-heartedness, as well as our joy and our wonderful, quivering aliveness. Then, we can be equally intimate with a tree, or a cloud, or another person. When we experience true intimacy with someone, we recognize their sacredness and their beauty. True intimacy naturally inspires respect and reverence.

We experience intimacy with God in two ways: on the one hand, God reveals him or herself to us through the world, which is God's body. So in this sense, intimacy with God means intimacy with the world. When you stroke your cat, you are stroking God. There's no separation. On the other hand, God also approaches us from within, as our heart's longing and as the tiny voice that whispers to the soul.

Mystics like to think of God as their lover. When you imagine God being your lover, you get a sense of how intimate that relationship could be. It's exciting, it's erotic, it crackles with electricity. We need to bring that erotic juice back into our spirituality.

All desire is ultimately the desire for happiness, bliss, and ecstasy. All desire is the desire to experience that rapture which the mystics speak of as sacred union, or the divine marriage. However, we all get caught up in some form of illusion. We think a particular man or woman will give us the bliss we seek – or maybe it's money, or success, or a drug.

Traditional religion often condemns these types of 'worldly' desires. They say, don't waste your time, go straight to God. I say that our quest for love, or money, or security is not a waste of time. Rather, it's the way we learn our spiritual lessons. It's how we acquire wisdom. At the same time, can we understand that through the lover, or the money, we are seeking something else, something otherworldly? We're after what the Sufis call the Beloved, or the Priceless Pearl.

Consumer society feeds only those desires that can be exploited for financial profit. It invites us to shop till we drop, and every day new credit cards arrive in the mail to egg us on. Meanwhile, the desires of the heart and the soul go unattended. Addictions and eating disorders run rampant. On the one hand we're raping the planet to satisfy our greed, on the other, we've put our hearts on a starvation diet. This is a great tragedy, and unless we begin to honor the desires of the soul, it can only lead to disaster.

The desires of the soul should take precedence over the desires of the ego. When you lie on your deathbed, you won't care whether you drove an expensive car, or had a prestigious job. What will matter to you is whether you lived your life fully, whether you loved deeply, and whether you did what your soul came here to do.

Walking Marriages

Yang Erche Namu, *Lake Lugu, Eastern Himalayas, China.*
Pop singer and author.

In our Moso language there are no words for husband, wife, jealousy or fidelity; women make all the decisions about who they go with and who they stay with. A man may be an *azhu*, a close male friend, but that's as close as we get to any form of marital obligation.

According to our tradition, a family should never divide. In the Moso culture, marriage is considered to be an attack on the family. We practice *zouhun*, 'walking marriage', in which a man and a woman may spend the night together, but he walks back to his own home in the morning.

Couples share neither ties nor possessions. We women inherit all the property and bring up the children, who grow up side by side with their cousins – the children of our mother's sisters. The only men who live in the house are our brothers and uncles. So in place of one father, Moso children have many uncles who take care of them.

Women and men should not marry, for love is like the seasons – it comes and goes.

Among my people this is how families live together.

The Role of a Lifetime

Michael Douglas, *USA.*
Actor, producer and UN Messenger of Peace.

It's hard to balance work and family. I work in an industry that has a relatively short window of opportunity, extremely long hours and can take you away from home for months at a time. The rewards can be fantastic: fame, wealth, artistic gratification, never standing in line for a table at a restaurant. But the guilt of shortchanging your family can gnaw away at you.

Hard work or being compulsive is something you may learn from family. My father has made 90 films. He did four to five a year when I was growing up. I missed him, and he was guilt-ridden for not being around. Today he's 90 years old, having just published his ninth book. I am filled with love and admiration for what he's accomplished. Not just in his career but in the way he has conducted himself in the third act of his life.

I'm going to be 63 this month. I've been married for seven years to an extraordinary woman 25 years younger than me, actress Catherine Zeta-Jones. We have two children, a daughter, 4, and a son, 7. To say my priorities have changed would be a gross understatement! My life is centered around my family's schedule. Our daughter, Carys, just started kindergarten and our son, Dylan, began the second grade last week. They are at a precious age, and I don't want to miss a minute of it. Like all parents, I labor to keep them on schedule, and try to teach them how to think positively and to work through daily life. I also strive to be sure they have fun. Carys is at the stage when she's discovered 'dress-up': purses, high heels – anything pink. Dylan is a big climber – rocks, mountains and trees. He loves the outdoors. I read with my kids every night. That has become a favorite for me.

We've moved to the island of Bermuda, where I spent a lot of time as a kid (my mother is Bermudian and still has a large family there.) I adjust my schedule to my wife's, since she is in the prime of her career. The school year tells us when we are going to travel. The kids know what Mommy does for a living, but they have never seen Daddy's movies (they're too young), so Mommy makes movies and Daddy makes pancakes! I don't really cook, but I am the take-out and home-delivery expert. I enjoy it. It's all given me great satisfaction. Don't get me wrong. I still go to work, but now only on projects I really care about. I have a new movie coming out called "King of California." We filmed it in only 31 days, not like some of the 90-day shooting schedules of the past.

I play a father who reconciles with his 17 year old daughter, played by Evan Rachel Wood. I understood and identified with the role. My oldest son from my first marriage, Cameron, who is 28, did not benefit from my new priorities. He was short-changed. Nevertheless he understands now, and he knows how much I love him.

I love being home. That feeling is based on a good marriage and having the time to spend with the kids. Age gives you experience to nurture a relationship. Not long ago, my father gave me some great advice. He loves giving advice now. He pointed toward Catherine and said, "When it's all over, all you really have is your wife. You can dote on your kids all you want, but they're going to grow up and leave you someday. Then it will be just the two of you." Many times people make more of an effort toward strangers than the people closest to them.

There is so much to learn in raising a family. So where are you going to find out how to do it, especially if you didn't benefit from proper role models? When I went to college at the University of California, Santa Barbara, in the 1960s, you could graduate with a degree in home economics. It was eventually disbanded largely due to politics and the power of the women's movement. I'm happy to see that "home ec" is currently being revived at some colleges.

I've reached an age when I start getting those questions – What do you want for your children? What do you see as your legacy? Oh, oh, mortality! I have good role models in my father and mother. Basically, you want to try to leave this earth having given more to it than having taken away. That makes you a good citizen of the planet. If I can pass this on from generation to generation, that's as close to immortality as I can hope to get.

Leafy Trees

Prof. Pan Guang, *People's Republic of China.*
Director of the Shanghai Center for International Studies, *Dean of the* Center of Jewish Studies, *Shanghai, and Vice-Chairman of the* Chinese Society of Middle East Studies.

Our life is the prolongation of that of our ancestors and we progress in it following their footsteps. In turn, the life of our successors is a prolongation of our own: when the shoot we plant becomes a leafy tree, they will be able to sit in the freshness of its shade.

In our life, we enjoy time and time again, those material and spiritual riches bequeathed to us from our ancestors, and especially the extremely valuable traditions which are passed down from generation to generation. As their descendants, we have the right to enjoy to the full all that has been left to us.

However, we shouldn't just limit ourselves to enjoying and handing down these riches and traditions, but we should also develop them on a daily basis and improve on them, so that we will be able to leave our own imprint on history.

If we think about this often, our existence will abound with vitality and we will become aware of the many things we still have left to do. And if we apply ourselves to the task with sincerity, we will feel happy and fulfilled when our life approaches its end, because not only will we have passed on to our descendants those riches and traditions which we've received from our ancestors, we will also have bequeathed them some of those treasures which we ourselves have created.

Reconciliation

Why Forgive?

Desmond Tutu, *South Africa.*
Former Archbishop of Cape Town and Chairman of South Africa's
Truth and Reconciliation Commission.

Malusi Mpumlwana was a young enthusiastic anti-apartheid activist and a close associate of Steve Biko in South Africa's crucial Black Consciousness Movement of the late 1970s and early 1980s. He was involved in vital community development and health projects with impoverished and often demoralized rural communities. As a result, he and his wife were under strict surveillance, constantly harassed by the ubiquitous security police. They were frequently held in detention without trial.

I remember well a day Malusi gave the security police the slip and came to my office in Johannesburg, where I was serving as general secretary of the South African Council of Churches. He told me that during his frequent stints in detention, when the security police routinely tortured him, he used to think, "These are God's children and yet they are behaving like animals. They need us to help them recover the humanity they have lost." For our struggle against apartheid to be successful, it required remarkable young people like Malusi.

All South Africans were less than whole because of apartheid. Blacks suffered years of cruelty and oppression, while many privileged whites became more uncaring, less compassionate, less humane, and therefore less human. Yet during these years of suffering and inequality, each South African's humanity was still tied to that of all others, white or black, friend or enemy. For our own dignity can only be measured in the way we treat others. This was Malusi's extraordinary insight.

I saw the power of this idea when I was serving as chairman of the Truth and Reconciliation Commission in South Africa. This was the commission that the post-apartheid government, headed by our president, Nelson Mandela, had established to move us beyond the cycles of retribution and violence that had plagued so many other countries during their transitions from oppression to democracy. The commission granted perpetrators of political crimes the opportunity to appeal for amnesty by giving a full and truthful account of their actions and, if they so chose, an opportunity to ask for forgiveness – opportunities that some took and others did not.

The commission also gave victims of political crimes a chance to tell their stories, hear confessions, and thus unburden themselves from the pain and suffering they had experienced.

For our nation to heal and become a more humane place, we had to embrace our enemies as well as our friends. The same is true the world over. True enduring peace – between countries, within a country, within a community, within a family – requires real reconciliation between former enemies and even between loved ones who have struggled with one another.

How could anyone really think that true reconciliation could avoid a proper confrontation? After a husband and wife or two friends have quarreled, if they merely seek to gloss over their differences or metaphorically paper over the cracks, they must not be surprised when they are soon at it again, perhaps more violently than before, because they have tried to heal their ailment lightly.

True reconciliation is based on forgiveness, and forgiveness is based on true confession, and confession is based on penitence, on contrition, on sorrow for what you have done. We know that when a husband and wife have quarreled, one of them must be ready to say the most difficult words in any language, "I'm sorry," and the other must be ready to forgive for there to be a future for their relationship. This is true between parents and children, between siblings, between neighbors, and between friends. Equally, confession, forgiveness, and reconciliation in the lives of nations are not just airy-fairy religious and spiritual things, nebulous and unrealistic. They are the stuff of practical politics.

Those who forget the past, as many have pointed out, are doomed to repeat it. Just in terms of human psychology, we in South Africa knew that to have blanket amnesty where no disclosure was made would not deal with our past. It is not dealing with the past to say glibly, "Let bygones be bygones," for then they will never be bygones. How can you forgive if you do not know what or whom to forgive? In our commission hearings, we required full disclosure for us to grant amnesty. Only then, we thought, would the process of requesting and receiving forgiveness be healing and transformative for all involved. The commission's record shows that its standards for disclosure and amnesty were high indeed: Of the more than 7,000 applications submitted to the Truth and Reconciliation Commission, it granted amnesty to only 849 of them.

Unearthing the truth was necessary not only for the victims to heal, but for the perpetrators as well. Guilt, even unacknowledged guilt, has a negative effect on the guilty. One day it will come out in some form or another. We must be radical. We must go to the root, remove that which is festering, cleanse and cauterize, and then a new beginning is possible.

Forgiveness gives us the capacity to make a new start. That is the power, the rationale, of confession and forgiveness. It is to say, "I have fallen but I am not going to remain there. Please forgive me." And forgiveness is the grace by which you enable the other person to get up, and get up with dignity, to begin anew. Not to forgive leads to bitterness and hatred, which just like self-hatred and self-contempt, gnaw away at the vitals of one's being. Whether hatred is projected out or projected in, it is always corrosive of the human spirit.

We have all experienced how much better we feel after apologies are made and accepted, but even still it is so hard for us to say that we are sorry. I often find it difficult to say these words to my wife in the intimacy and love of our bedroom. How much more difficult it is to say these words to our friends, our neighbors, and our co-workers. Asking for forgiveness requires that we take responsibility for our part in the rupture that has occurred in the relationship. We can always make excuses for ourselves and find justifications for our actions, however contorted, but we know that these keep us locked in the prison of blame and shame.

In the story of Adam and Eve, the Bible reminds us of how easy it is to blame others. When God confronted Adam about eating the forbidden fruit from the Tree of Knowledge of Good and Evil, Adam was less than forthcoming in accepting responsibility. Instead he shifted the blame to Eve, and when God turned to Eve, she too tried to pass the buck to the serpent. (The poor serpent had no one left to blame.) So we should not be surprised at how reluctant most people are to acknowledge their responsibility and to say they are sorry. We are behaving true to our ancestors when we blame everyone and everything except ourselves. It is the everyday heroic act that says, "It's my fault. I'm sorry." But without these simple words, forgiveness is much more difficult.

Forgiving and being reconciled to our enemies or our loved ones are not about pretending that things are other than they are. It is not about patting one another on the back and turning a blind eye to the wrong. True reconciliation exposes the awfulness, the abuse, the pain, the hurt, the truth. It could even sometimes make things worse. It is a risky undertaking but in the end it is worthwhile, because in the end only an honest confrontation with reality can bring real healing. Superficial reconciliation can bring only superficial healing.

If the wrongdoer has come to the point of realizing his wrong, then one hopes there will be contrition, or at least some remorse or sorrow. This should lead him to confess the wrong he has done and ask for forgiveness. It obviously requires a fair measure of humility. But what happens when such contrition or confession is lacking? Must the victim be dependent on these before she can forgive? There is no question that such a confession is a very great help to the one who wants to forgive, but it is not absolutely indispensable. If the victim could forgive only when the culprit confessed, then the victim would be locked into the culprit's whim, locked into victimhood, no matter her own attitude or intention. That would be palpably unjust.

In the act of forgiveness, we are declaring our faith in the future of a relationship and in the capacity of the wrongdoer to change. We are welcoming a chance to make a new beginning. Because we are not infallible, because we will hurt especially the ones we love by some wrong, we will always need a process of forgiveness and reconciliation to deal with those unfortunate yet all too human breaches in relationships. They are an inescapable characteristic of the human condition.

We have had a jurisprudence, a penology in Africa that was not retributive but restorative. Traditionally, when people quarreled, the main intention was not to punish the miscreant but to restore good relations. This was the animating principle of our Truth and Reconciliation Commission. For Africa is concerned, or has traditionally been concerned, about the wholeness of relationships. That is something we need in this world – a world that is polarized, a world that is fragmented, a world that destroys people. It is also something we need in our families and friendships. For retribution wounds and divides us from one another. Only restoration can heal us and make us whole. And only forgiveness enables us to restore trust and compassion to our relationships. If peace is our goal, there can be no future without forgiveness.

The Art of Peacemaking

Eliyahu McLean, *Israel.*
Rodef Shalom, *or Peacemaker in the Jewish tradition, co-director of* Jerusalem Peacemakers, *and pioneer of several interfaith projects for Israeli-Palestinian reconciliation.*

In our increasingly polarized world, traditional Jewish teachings about peace can offer us wisdom that we can apply in our current predicament. The word *shalom* in Hebrew means peace. From the same root in Hebrew comes the word *shalem*, or wholeness.

The great Hassidic philosopher Rebbe Nachman taught that the highest, or absolute, peace is the peace between opposites. That is, it is our task to seek the unity in the opposites, to seek to bring wholeness within ourselves and to our families, communities and nations.

The real significance of peace is to join opposites. We shouldn't be troubled when we come across someone who is our exact opposite and whose thoughts are contrary to our own. Neither should we conclude that we will never be able to live together harmoniously. The laws of physics dictate that opposites attract. Absolute peace is achieved through the effort to make peace between opposites, just as *Hashem* – Hebrew for 'The Name', or God – makes peace in His High Places between fire and water, which are also opposing forces. In our work in the Holy Land we have brought together Jewish, Christian, Muslim and Druze religious leaders, in a group called 'The Abrahamic Reunion'. We jointly issued 'A Call for Reconciliation' after the Lebanon war to show cooperation among the faiths by example, and that our destiny is to live together as one family.

In this and many other gatherings for prayer and dialogue, we have succeeded in bringing together many Palestinians and Israelis who otherwise would have seen each other as enemies. The atmosphere of both safety and unity at our gatherings helps to re-build trust between opposing national and religious communities. In this process we come to re-humanize 'the other' and to take down the walls of fear that separate us.

The ancient Jewish sage Hillel taught us in the *Pirkei Avot*, or 'Ethics of the Fathers', to be like the disciples of Aaron, loving peace and pursuing peace. If we define peace, *shalom*, as *shalem* – seeking wholeness – then wherever we live, we should seek to become a bridge between different worlds. We can bring awareness to people and situations that may seem to oppose each other on one (political, social, religious) level, yet resonate together on a deeper, perhaps hidden level.

My teacher Rabbi Shlomo Carlebach, always taught that we should wear our *Moshiach*, or Messiah glasses, at all times, that is, to see the world through the eyes of the Messiah, not just to see the world as it is, broken, but how it has the potential to be mended … to see the potential for healing, transformation, and wholeness in every situation.

The Way of Aloha

Wayne Kealohi Powell, *Hawai'i.*
Shamanic instructor and Alaka'i, *or Guide, of the* Order of Huna International.

The word *Hawai'i* is not only the name of several islands in the middle of the Pacific Ocean, it is also the name of an ancient people. As all Hawai'ian words are conceptual in nature and have many meanings, what they mean is determined by the context in which they are used.

Breaking the word *Hawai'i* down into some of its root meanings, *Ha* is the sacred breath of the creation of life; *wai* is the holy water that sustains life and is also a symbol of great abundance, while *i* emphasizes that which came before it.

Therefore, a very simplified translation of *Hawai'i* is 'an abundance of the forces that create and sustain life' – within my people and our islands called Hawai'i, and *Aloha* is our way of life.

Living *Aloha* is a way of life that all the great masters have taught us in their own language throughout time. The problem is that we have all been trained to respond to things as warriors rather than with *Aloha*. "The world is a dangerous place," is the root belief of the warrior. "The world is a loving place" is the belief of *Aloha*.

The Way of Aloha is a path that emphasizes acceptance, forgiveness and co-operation through the development of hyper-awareness, the cultivation of *Mana* – inner power – friendship and unity, the practice of survival and exploration skills, and an ethic of 'love and be loved.' The typical ideal is to act in such a way as to get the best results for everyone in any given situation, with the emphasis on enjoyment and creating peace and harmony.

Essential to creating a life of loving co-operation is the idea of *Kahi* – Oneness. To practice *Aloha*, we need to give up our deeply-rooted assumption that "we are all separate," in order to feel our inner connections with all people, places and things. If a hunter felt his inner connection with the deer or any other wild life, he could not kill it. If a logger felt his inner connection to the trees, he would not slaughter them.

It's this belief that we are all separate that enables us to dump raw sewage into our beloved oceans, and spill each other's blood in wars, fighting over boundaries or differences of religious beliefs. Hate and war are our ultimate mis-creations, because they go against the basic truth of our abundance in all that we are, all that we have and aganst our most basic human needs: to love and be loved, which is the spiritual law of *Aloha*.

The Way of Aloha can be practised and experienced anywhere, anytime and with anyone. It is a path of love, harmony and appreciation for the beauty in all things and people, and is available only in this eternal moment of now.

Art

CALLIGRAPHY

Parvin Heydari Nassab, *Iran.*
Islamic illuminator and calligrapher. The first female instructor at the
Iran School of Calligraphy, *Tehran.*

Calligraphy is the moment in which the harsh heat of the desert, the strivings of our peoples, the thoughts and apprehensions of the Orient, the harmony of sensibility and meditation, are all made manifest on the blank page, to reveal a message of divine love and earthly beauty.

This calligraphic journey of mine has its point of departure on a road that begins at the very edge of the page and ends in a whirl of twists and turns. In itself, it can unravel the mystery inherent in the erotic plea of Persian poetry, and, by a juxtapostion of black and white, channels the words into unadulterated black, a black that contains within itself a world of contrasts, hallucinatory and secretive, to terminate in a state of absolute beauty. Patience, endurance, repetition on the battlefield in which the words take shape and form, bring hand and mind together in a unique and harmonious tapestry, permitting the dancing pen to flow over the white bedrock of the page with its message of life.

Calligraphy and I have always been like water flowing across the Earth's surface, coursing over plains and plants, peaks and people, bearing our message and spreading love and friendship along the way.

Flowing like water.

Origami

David Lister, *England.*
Origami historian and founding member of the British Origami Society.

"He showed me a little thing the size of a hazelnut in the palm of my hand, and it was as round as a ball. I looked at it with my mind's eye and thought, 'What can this be?' And the answer came, 'It is all that is made."

Dame Julian of Norwich (born 1342)

One would think, at first sight, that there would be little connection between spiritual values and paperfolding. Paperfolding is essentially just a hobby or a craft; perhaps, even, an art. How can recreational manipulation of paper possibly have spiritual values?

However, if we consider the matter in more general terms, it is wholly accepted that paperfolding as we practise it in mainstream origami is firmly based in geometry. Mathematics determines its every form and process. And does not mathematics disclose the very Mind of God?

I place an ordinary piece of square origami paper before me. What do I see? At one level I see no more than a piece of paper, a thin compression of plant fibres. But what else do I see? I see the square of paper twisting and turning itself until the semblance of a bird emerges from the paper to stand before me.

And then the bird dissolves again and I am left with my original sheet of paper, now seemingly imprinted with crease lines which form a curious geometrical pattern. Is the bird or its form still residing there in the paper? Was it there before the paper took the shape of the bird? Did it exist as a Platonic idea? Or do these ideas exist only in my own mind? But surely I did not invent the mathematical patterns. Where did they come from if not from God?

Vittorio-Maria Brandoni, who founded a school of origami based on Zen principles, believed that origami should not just express an 'empty aestheticism', but rather, an attitude to life and nature.

Just as the practice of contemplation in Zen leads to enlightenment, so folding in the right way should lead to a 'waking up' of our minds and hearts. But, he adds, origami is only folding paper – he who wants to understand it just has to start.

So, once more, I look at the plain square of paper in front of me. And I find that it is no longer a mere piece of paper. I find that it is a magic casement through which I can gaze at enchanted landscapes and pass to worlds of a higher experience. So, I recall the words of William Blake:

"*To see a World in a grain of sand, and Heaven in a wildflower, hold infinity in the palm of your hand, and eternity in an hour.*"

Blake's words are an echo of those of Dame Julian with which I began this piece. Is not our grain of sand, our hazelnut, just a simple square of paper?

Why Literature?

Mario Vargas Llosa, *Peru.*
Writer and novelist.

We live in an era of knowledge specialisation, due to the prodigious development of science and technology, and the fragmentation of knowledge into innumerable paths and compartments, a cultural trend that will only be accentuated in years to come. Of course, specialisation brings great benefits, offering much more detailed research and experimentation; it is the engine of progress. But it also has a negative effect: it elides all those common denominators of culture through which men and women co-exist, communicate and feel a sense of solidarity.

Specialisation leads to a lack of social communication, to the division of people into cultural ghettoes of technicians and specialists. They share a language, codes and information that are increasingly specialised and specific, which limits them in a way that the old proverb has warned us against: they can't see the wood for the trees.

And knowing that the wood exists is what binds a society together and prevents it from collapsing into a myriad of solipsistic parts. And solipsism – in nations or in individuals – produces paranoia and delirium, those disfigurements of reality that can cause hatred, wars and genocide.

In our day and age, science and technology are increasingly divorced from broader culture, precisely because of the infinite complexity of its knowledge and the speed of its evolution, which has led to specialisation and the use of hermetic language.

Literature, by contrast, is, has been, and will continue to be for as long as it exists, one of the common denominators of human existence through which human beings recognise themselves and talk to each other, no matter how different their professions or their plans for life, their geographical location, their individual circumstances or the historical moment that they are living in.

Those of us who read Cervantes, Shakespeare, Dante or Tolstoy understand each other and feel part of the same species because, in the works that these writers created, we learn what we share as human beings, what is common in all of us beneath the wide range of differences that separate us. And there is no better defence against the stupidity of prejudice, racism, xenophobia, religious or political sectarianism or autarkic nationalism than this invariable truth that appears in all great literature: that men and women from across the world are equal, and that it is unjust that they are subject to discrimination, repression and exploitation.

Nothing teaches us better than literature to see, in ethnic and cultural differences, the richness of our shared heritage, and to prize these differences as a demonstration of our diverse creativity. Reading good literature is enjoyable, of course; but we also learn, in that direct and intense way that we experience life through fictions, what and how we are, our human integrity, our actions and dreams and fantasies, alone or in the dense web of relations that link us to others, in our public persona and in the intimacy of our consciousness, that complex sum of contrary truths – in the words of Isaiah Berlin – that make up the human condition.

Life

The Art of Living

Sir Richard Branson, *England.*
Entrepreneur and founder of The Virgin Group.

Living life to the full is an often-used but misunderstood expression, but one which I truly believe in. To me there is no easy excuse for the words "can't be done" uttered so often by people who really mean "I don't want to do it and I don't want to bother to find out if it can be done".

We only have one life and I strongly feel that every day that we live is precious time … be it spent with family, friends or working with colleagues, and have always believed that separating the work side of living from the relaxation of recreation, fun and family is too rigid a divide if one wants to be successful in the art of living. I include my family in my work and for that reason I suppose my wife, Joan, has long been my closest advisor and sounding-board about ideas, people and issues that one has to face in daily life. I often take my family with me when I have to travel with my work and they also know many of my colleagues as well. This actually helps to reduce the stress of a fairly hectic schedule and lifestyle.

It is also important to be true to one's beliefs and ideas, and here is an example: before the last Gulf War I became convinced that someone of the stature of Nelson Mandela might be able to persuade Saddam Hussein to abdicate power if he could be convinced that the U.S. really would invade, and provide compelling non-political persuasion quietly away from the crescendo rhetoric of both sides as the conflict approached. Saddam promised "the mother of all battles" as the U.S. prepared to "shock and awe" us in front of our TVs. Sadly, the plane was on the runway in South Africa ready to go, but the invasion pipped our "can't be done" idea to the post.

Good has come of that thought and Nelson Mandela has now put together a group of former world leaders and advisors, called The Elders, that I am privileged to support in their mission to be prepared to intervene in situations and world issues without the baggage of entrenched political positions, and so allowing them to work behind the scenes where today's politicians are unable to. Maybe "it can't be done" but here is a group that can at least try before it is too late, and that to me is the art of living!

On a lighter note, we should never forget that the art of living a long and happy life is best achieved by following that old saying, "Treat others as you would expect to be treated yourself." I think we rarely stop to think about what this really means. I try to never lose my temper, I hate it when people lose theirs with me and it makes you wonder how the angry person screaming at check-in staff or on the end of the phone to a call centre possibly imagines they are achieving more than the calm and friendly voice that explains the problem that needs dealing with.

I would have thought that there is more than enough evidence that aggressive, stressed and angry individuals die younger, to have persuaded them to count to ten before launching on the next hopeless crusade, aimed only at inflicting the same misery on others that they clearly feel themselves.

So the art of living may be as simple as learning to count a few heartbeats of time before turning a thought into speech.

I am also a firm believer in praising those around me even when I feel the need to criticise, and I also think people should be encouraged to follow their dreams, even if that entails persuading them to throw themselves into what they do with a positive attitude for now, and to pursue the dream in their spare time.

Perhaps the art of living is best described by the French philosopher and scientist, Henri Poincaré: "The scientist does not study nature because it is useful; he studies it because he delights in it, and he delights in it because it is beautiful. If nature were not beautiful, it would not be worth knowing, and if nature were not worth knowing, life would not be worth living."

'Still Here'

Dr. Jean Shinoda Bolen, *San Francisco, USA.*
Psychiatrist, Jungian analyst and author of The Millionth Circle.

No matter what the cause, every time death comes to others, whether gently or like a Tsunami and we are spared, there is an inner felt affirmation that "I am still here." Even in grief and mourning or guilt that "it should have been me," there is this reality, "I am still here." The challenge is to find or have the sense that there is meaning and purpose to being alive. If we are – as I believe – spiritual beings on a human path, it means that there is still more for us to experience, to do, to learn, or to love if we are still here.

Implicitly believed is that each of us has a soul. This means that something immortal has become embodied in each of us for a relatively short time. Each of us arrives as a vulnerable, dependent infant into the world, which is imperfect, dysfunctional, sometimes even terrifying. Encountering disappointment, betrayal, abandonment, limitation, is to be expected: suffering of one sort or another comes with life. Power to inflict pain on another or take advantage of another comes our way as well.

While this is so, the human experience offers opportunities to love and be loved, to feel awe and be moved by beauty, to make mistakes, to choose how we respond to what happens to us, to grow in compassion and wisdom, and to contribute by who we become to the sum of human potential.

The magnus opus each of us has is the life we have. Like a canvas, a manuscript, or music being improvised, while we are still here, the work is not yet finished. To be human is to intuitively know or to live with the possibility that we have some significance in a vast visible and invisible universe. Living from this premise, I believe that what we do here does matter and that someday, we *will* know.

On Living as an Art Form

Prof. Dr. Mehmet Aydin, *Republic of Turkey.*
Theologian & Minister of State.

When I turn to my inner world and ask myself, "What is the meaning of life?", it is the word 'synthesis' which most often comes to my mind. As long as it isn't forced, synthesis takes place alongside a kind of balance.

A 'beautiful' life is the synthesis of all of life's major experiences. We are beings who 'know', who 'believe'; we are imbued with moral values and an appreciation of beauty. In other words, it is, to a large extent, the cognitive, religious-inner-spiritual, moral and aesthetic experiences which bestow meaning on our lives.

What makes living an art form is when these experiences reach that state – or level of being – where there is 'unity in diversity', where they support and nourish each other without losing their own partial autonomy.

I know this is not easy. In my opinion, what matters here is to be 'en route towards the destination', and, therefore, to experience 'getting closer'. And rather than an 'event', this experience is a 'happening', a process.

History teaches us that it is possible to transmit a large part of our human experience to other people. The existence of mutual influences, overlapping, similarities, and even differences between cultures and civilizations testifies to this fact. Whatever the objections which some thinkers may come up with, in the final analysis, there is only one humanity occupying this earth.

And humanity today faces a serious threat. This is revealed in the way that, on the one hand, cognitive experiences have been subjugated, to a great extent, to the rule of sheer force; moral experiences have been relativized to the point of weakening this unity; aesthetic experience devoid of any sensitivity has become a matter of money, and spirituality has been demoted, to a large extent, to the level of mere esotericism.

Meanwhile, a 'culturalism', and even a 'civilizationism' have emerged, which feed separation, division and fragmentation. And this has led to the attitude of, "I am equipped with civilized values, therefore the 'other' must follow my path." Today, it is this very same attitude which is the foremost enemy of living in harmony, or of 'unity in diversity'.

There is a way out of this dilemma. There are many values which humanity possesses which can be described as being universal, and in today's world, human rights cannot be overridden by the beliefs of any one given culture. There may be different cultural interpretations and even applications of these rights and values, provided they do not jeopardize these values' quintessential elements, and their universal recognizability.

My belief is that if we are able to gather round these values and cherish those of our differences which do not clash with them, we will have taken a very important step to regarding human life as an art form.

Living

Dr. Ismail Serageldin, *Egypt.*
Director of the Alexandria Library, *the world's first library and research centre.*

To be one with nature, with the universe and with all people. To rejoice in being human, and to cherish the capacity to think. To care for this wonderful world and to try to do something to leave it better than we found it. To be able to honor the past, to celebrate the present and to embrace the future. To be able to shout with joy and conviction:

> The world is my home.
> Humanity is my family,
> Non-violence is my creed.
> Peace, justice, equality and dignity for all is my purpose.
> Engagement, rationality, tolerance, dialogue, learning and understanding are my means.

To welcome with outstretched hands all those who share these beliefs ... that, for me, is the art of living.

Healing

Laura Weaver, *Colorado, USA.*
Program Director of PassageWorks Institute, *NGO dedicated to nourishing the inner lives of young people through school-based rites of passage programs.*

It was a day in February – a day like any other day. Cold, clear skies blazing behind the Rocky Mountains. People sipping coffee in cafés. Toddlers laughing on park swings. And an MRI film on a screen before me, showing a large tumor in my pituitary gland. Benign, the doctor said. But the tumor was pushing against my pituitary stalk, driving upwards towards my optic nerves, and edging towards my carotid arteries. Something shifted in me. I was facing a major health crisis, and I was only 35 years old.

Then came the hours of research. The grieving. The begging. The pleading. The hoping for miracles. The months of alternative therapies, only to find that, a year later, the tumor had grown, not diminished. I was facing my biggest fear – brain surgery. I was going to have to stare into the face of illness and vulnerability and death and say yes, I will go there, because there is no other choice.

Emerging from the anesthesia, I was ecstatic. I had made it, survived – and I had felt held, truly cradled by a force much greater than myself. I sighed with relief – the ordeal was over. Slowly, life resumed. I worked, wrote, laughed, cooked. I held my children closer, breathed them in like the rarest air. Slowly I returned, stepping back into the flow of the speedy world, and life became common again.

A year later, another MRI in hand, I listened as the doctor announced that the tumor had quickly regrown. Lightning had struck twice, and I was blown open by the force of it. Again I replayed the scene: the down-on-the-knees praying, the bargaining – *I'll do anything but this.* But here it was. My hand to play.

"Alright," I said, "I will do it again, because I must, and because the obstacles that come to us are the teachers we have – no matter how unjust or unwelcome they feel." And so I underwent a second, more complex, more invasive surgery and came through it unscathed to the other side.

Now I am two months into my recovery, I see that healing is not just about illness or crisis. Healing is a life path – one we are walking, whether we notice or not, whether we like it or not.

Each day, there is the mystery. There are no guarantees. We simply never know. We are made humble again and again by the complexity of this exquisite planet, the intricacies of our own bodies, the spiraling of galaxies in deep space. And yet we forget. Over and over, we forget.

Eight weeks out from surgery, and already I have to remind myself to see, to really see – to listen to the rush of the snowmelt in the creek, follow the flickering light filtered through pines, trace the whirling patterns of snowflakes, breathe the scent of my lover's hair, stroke my children's soft faces. It is simple really. This luminous moment is all we have. And truly, it is all I have ever wanted.

Life Is Beautiful

Alice Herz-Sommer, *Prague, Czech Republic.*
Concert pianist and Holocaust survivor. 104-years-old.

When you know history – wars and wars and wars … it begins with this: that we are born half-good and half-bad – everybody, everybody. And there are situations where the bad comes out and situations where the good comes out. This is the reason why people invented religion, I believe. I had a twin sister – same mother, same father, same upbringing. She was extremely gifted, but a terrible pessimist, but I was the contrary. This is the reason I am so old, even now, I am sure. I am looking for the nice things in life. I know about the bad things, but I look only for the good things.

The world is wonderful, it's full of beauty and full of miracles. Our brain, the memory, how does it work? Not to speak of art and music … it is a miracle.

When I came back home after the Second World War, it was very, very painful because nobody else came back. My husband, the whole family of my husband, several members of my family, all my friends, all the friends of my family, nobody came back. It was a hard time. Then I realised what Hitler had done.

I never spoke a word about it because I didn't want my child to grow up with hatred because hatred breeds hatred. I succeeded. My son had very good friends in Germany and they invited him to play and they appreciated him. And I never hated, either, *never.*

I don't need religion. I understand when we are in a terrible situation we need hope. Religion, for me, is a symbol of hope. It helps, this hope. I know about religion, but even in the darkest times I never believed.

I love work. Work is the best invention, the best. Playing the piano is still a discipline. It makes you happy to have something. The worst thing is boredom. Boredom is dangerous.

I have never met anyone of this age. Never. When I was young, somebody of 60 was regarded as an old man. My temperament, this optimism and this discipline have enabled me to survive.

In any case, life is beautiful, extremely beautiful. And when you are old you appreciate it more. When you are older you think, you remember, you care and you appreciate. You are thankful for everything. Everything.

Death

Death

Huston Smith, *USA.*
Philosopher, theologian & author of The World's Religions.

Death is the most important question of our time … in good part because we refuse to face it.

Impermanence

Sogyal Rinpoche, *Tibet.*
Buddhist teacher & founder and spiritual director of Rigpa, *international network of Buddhist centers. Author of* The Tibetan Book of Living and Dying.

Death is a vast mystery, but there are two things we can say about it: It is absolutely certain that we will die, and it is uncertain when or how we will die. The only surety we have, then, is this uncertainty about the hour of our death, which we seize on as the excuse to postpone facing death directly. We are like children who cover their eyes in a game of hide-and-seek and think that no one can see them.

For all its technological achievements, modern Western society has no real understanding of death or what happens in death or after death. People today are taught to deny death, and taught that it means nothing but annihilation and loss. That means that most of the world lives either in denial of death or in terror of it. Even talking about death is considered morbid, and many people believe that simply mentioning death is to risk wishing it upon themselves.

All the greatest spiritual traditions in the world have told us clearly, that death is not the end. They have all handed down a vision of some sort of life to come, one which infuses this life that we are leading now with sacred meaning.

But despite their teachings, modern society is largely a spiritual desert, where the majority of people imagine that this life is all that there is.

According to the wisdom of Buddha, we can actually use our lives to prepare for death. We do not have to wait for the painful death of someone close to us or the shock of terminal illness to force us into looking at our lives. Nor are we condemned to go out empty-handed at death to meet the unknown. We can begin, here and now, to find meaning in our lives. We can make of every moment an opportunity to change and to prepare – wholeheartedly, precisely, and with peace of mind – for death and eternity.

In the Buddhist approach, life and death are seen as one whole, where death is the beginning of another chapter of life. Death is a mirror in which the entire meaning of life is reflected.

One of the chief reasons we have so much anguish and difficulty in facing death is that we ignore the truth of impermanence. We so desperately want everything to continue as it is that we have to believe that things will always stay the same. But this is only make-believe. And as we so often discover, belief has little or nothing to do with reality. This make-believe, with its misinformation, ideas, and assumptions, is the rickety foundation on which we construct our lives. No matter how much the truth keeps interrupting, we prefer to go on trying, with hopeless bravado, to keep up our pretense.

In our minds, changes always equal loss and suffering. And if they come, we try to anesthetize ourselves as far as possible. We assume, stubbornly and unquestioningly, that permanence provides security, and impermanence does not. But, in fact, impermanence is like some of the people we meet in life – difficult and disturbing at first, but on deeper acquaintance, far friendlier and less unnerving than we could have imagined.

The realization of impermanence is paradoxically the only thing we can hold onto, perhaps our only lasting possession. It is like the sky, or the earth. No matter how much everything around us may change or collapse, they endure. Say we go through a shattering emotional crisis … our whole life seems to be disintegrating … our husband or wife suddenly leaves us without warning. The earth is still there; the sky is still there. Of course, even the earth trembles now and again, just to remind us we cannot take anything for granted …

The cells of our body are dying, the neurons in our brain are decaying, even the expression on our face is always changing, depending on our mood. What we call our basic character is only a 'mindstream', nothing more. Today we feel good because things are going well; tomorrow we feel the opposite. Where did that good feeling go? New influences took us over as circumstances changed: we are impermanent, the influences are impermanent, and there is nothing solid or lasting anywhere that we can point to.

The only thing we really have is nowness, is now.

The Call to Perfection

Imam Feisal Abdul Rauf, *Kuwait.*
Chairman of The Cordoba Initiative, *an independent, non-partisan, interreligious project that works to improve Muslim-West relations, and Imam of Masjid al-Farah Mosque, New York.*

We are called to Perfection in the Divine Plan.

Life is a pilgrimage of our spirits through the harsh desert of this world, wandering, feeling uprooted and longing to return to the realm of light and life, from where they came and to which they shall return.

We therefore owe it to our souls to commit to a struggle along the path of God, that our souls may return to It in the highest degree of spiritual accomplishment – perfection.

This is the most important and fundamental octave in the art of living. Without recognition of this, our souls will eternally thirst.

How may we humans, fundamentally imperfect, heed this call? Don't our transgressions fill our world with grief and diminish our chances for eternal life? Struggling towards perfection – let alone attaining it – is hard work.

We must draw on two sources of inner strength that will help us on our journey: courage and self-discovery, for self-discovery is the key to God-discovery.

The Sufi aphorism, "Die before you die", is another instructive key which is critical in our attempts at courage and self-discovery.

Firstly, it means not waiting until we die, or are close to death, before we start thinking of God and looking for the Divine. The spiritual person rejects passivity and proactively seeks the Creator in all his or her worldly actions, for God as the very definition of Perfection is to be actively sought-after.

Secondly, "Dying before we die" means to destroy all that is bad and unworthy in ourselves, to develop higher and more refined skills, and to fathom the lines of the Divine that shape the inner dynamics of our lives.

Through this struggle, we will discover and develop capacities within ourselves that we didn't know existed. Just as the stars tranquilly follow their orbits in the sky, so we will grow towards our goal in harmony with the rhythm of the cosmos. Our equilibrium and peace will be great, for we will discover the justice of the Great Law in everything and everyone. We will be able to follow the invisible thread from human to human, from life to life, with our equilibrium unshaken, unshakable, and our joy unclouded.

Thirdly, it provides us with the courage to approach death – an accomplishment vital to living life more fully and perfectly. Not the courage of the brave biting their lips or facing death with a stoic stare, but with the courage of a wise person who recognizes death as a transition to a certain and better future, shaped by his or her worldly ethics.

Having eradicated the fear of death within ourselves, we will know suffering and adversity simply as *required* challenges on our variegated ways toward perfection. We will be able to tolerate suffering with equanimity because we are aware of its transience, so it does not asphyxiate us with fear. Understanding attenuates fear, and while fear may never abandon us entirely, through our spiritual struggle with suffering and joy, we can embrace that which we fear and come nearer to our goal – perfection.

And so we praise and thank God!

Remembering

Gloria Gilmartin, *Wisconsin, USA.*

Senior citizen and avid journal-writer, I enjoy the company of two dogs, one cat, one bird and a couple of goldfish. The mosaic of my life has been enriched by the experience of grieving.

On the first anniversary of my husband's death, I found myself dreading the approach of 10.26 pm.

How will I feel? What am I supposed to feel? What if I don't feel anything?

Over and over, all day long, these questions went through my head.

I thought of how quickly a year had passed. What had seemed like a dream and a nightmare twelve months earlier was actually beginning to resemble reality.

Grieving is a phenomenon. The hardest and most painful times pop up unexpectedly. Minutes without a painful twinge or thought of him occasionally have extended into hours. I am learning to accept these times as good, as normal, and to be grateful when these healing lapses of conscious grieving occur.

There still are times when I forget myself and think of how much Joe will enjoy hearing about something silly I did or find myself hoping he'll tell me that he's seen my misplaced keys. Jarred into remembering that he is no longer here to consult about this, that, or any other thing, I shake my head and question my sanity.

I have learned a lot about myself in this past year. I now accept that I am not as strong as I thought about certain things and that I am much more capable than ever regarding others.

What stands out most prominently is the gift of closeness that emerged between us in the last weeks of his life. Never in the time that I knew him was this man so honest and open or grateful. Every barrier came down as his spirit prepared to depart this life. No longer were there any pretenses or walls between us. He looked into my eyes with an honest, open vulnerability that he had never before been able to reveal. As weak and feeble as his body was, I saw a strength in his eyes that allowed me to see past any misgivings, annoyances and angers of yesterday. They just did not matter; to either of us.

What became significant was that this soul, this child of the Almighty, was soon to depart on a journey to another place, a place of Love and total acceptance. He needed my support through this stage of his journey and I needed to allow him to leave this world in peace and serenity.

I am grateful that the passing of time is allowing our happy memories to seize the spotlight and take center stage. A deeper understanding of love is replacing the pain of loss. When a person leaves this life, time does not stand still and love does not die. Love continues and grows. All that dies and fades is that which really did not matter.

What remains is the memory of joy; of the good times. What remains is the honor it was to hold his hand at 10.26 pm.

A reflection written in memory of Joseph F. Gilmartin.

A Place

John Berger, *England.*
Storyteller, essayist, novelist, screenwriter, dramatist and critic. Author of Ways of Seeing.

What reconciles me to my own death more than anything else is the image of a place: a place where your bones and mine are buried, thrown, uncovered, together. They are strewn there pell-mell. One of your ribs leans against my skull. A metacarpal of my left hand lies inside your pelvis. (Against my broken ribs your breast like a flower.) The hundred bones of our feet are scattered like gravel. It is strange that this image of our proximity, concerning as it does mere phosphate of calcium, should bestow a sense of peace. Yet it does. With you, I can imagine a place where to be phosphate of calcium is enough.

Japanese Death Poem

Shinsui, *Japan.*
Zen monk, died 9th September, 1769, at the age of 49.

A centuries-old Japanese tradition among Zen monks and Haiku poets is the jisei, *or death poem, written when on the verge of dying; the idea being that in the final moments of life, these thoughts on death are especially lucid and so are also important reflections on life.*

During his last moments, Shinsui's followers requested that he write a death poem. He grasped his brush, painted the following *(overleaf)*, and died.